SUPREME COURT'S AOR EXAM- LEADING CASES

CASE NOTES & SUMMERY OF 64 LEADING CASES FOR PAPER IV

JAYPRAKASH BANSILAL SOMANI

ISBN 979-888521449-0

Dedicated

To

All the Past & Present Judges of the Supreme Court of India.

Salute to their wisdom.

Salute to their interpretation of Law.

Salute to their elaborative judgement writing.

• • •

Contents

Contents

Contents

Contents

Contents

Preface

Dear Learned Aspirant Advocates for AOR Examination of the Supreme Court of India, Advocate of Supreme Court, High Courts, Tribunals & Trial Courts,

I am very delighted to provide you a book on **'Supreme Court's AOR Exam- Leading Cases'**

In this book you will get case notes & summery of all 64 leading case laws for Paper IV.

These are the landmark judgements, which are very important in the practice of the Supreme Court & all the High Courts & in the Tribunals also. Purpose of this book is to give in precise centralised idea of each case with majour principals of law applied & decision given by Hon'ble Judges of the Supreme Court of India.

My special thanks to Supreme Court Law Reports, Manupatra & Supreme Court website because of their support I can compile this book in well manner. I am also thankful to Notion Press to support me to publish & market this book throughout the Country. Thanks to my Juniors, Advocate Colleagues & Insolvency Professional Colleagues to support me in this venture.

Miss Aqsa Sahar has helped me a lot to compile this book.

I hope this book will add some value addition in the wealth of your legal knowledge. Your positive feedbacks will boost me to compile/ write further books & negative feedbacks will improve my skills. Kindly send your valuable feedbacks by email.

Thanks with Regards,

Jayprakash B. Somani

Advocate, Supreme Court of India

Email: jaysomani64@gmail.com

Web Site: www.jayprakashsomani.com

Call: 8384051134, 9322188701, 9318381287

Acknowledgements

Printed & Published by
Notion Press
No. 8, 3rd Cross Street,
CIT Colony, Mylapore,
Chennai, Tamil Nadu- 600004

• • •

Managed by
Jayprakash Somani Advocates & Solicitors
Law Firm for Supreme Court of India
Delhi Office
257 C, Pocket 1, Mayur Vihar Phase 1, Delhi 110091.
Call 8384051134, 9322188701, 8459194576, 9318381287
01141051516
Supreme Court Chamber
312, 3rd Floor, M. C. Setalvad Block, In front of 'D' Gate, Bhagwan Das Road, Supreme Court of India, New Delhi 110001
Contact: 8459194576, 9811011747,
www.jayprakashsomani.com

• • •

Books are available online at
1. Notion Press: https://notionpress.com/author/jayprakash_somani
2. Amazon: https://www.amazon.in/s?k=jayprakash+somani
3. Flipkart: https://www.flipkart.com/search?q=Jayprakash%20Somani

• • •

CHAPTER I

HIS HOLINESS KESAVANANDA BHARATI SRIPADAGALA VARU Vs. STATE OF KERALA April 24, 1973

Citations: [1973] Suppl. SCR 1, (1973) 4 SCC 225

(S. M. SIKRI, C. J., J. M. SHELAT, K. S. HEGDE, A. N. GROVER, A. N. RAY, P. JAGANMOHAN REDDY, D. G.

PALEKAR, H. R. KHANNA, IC K. MATHEW, M. H. BEG, S. N. DWIVEDI, A. K. MUKHERJEA AND Y. V.

CHANDRACHUD, JJ.)

Constitution of India, 1950-Artick 368 before Constitution (Twenty Fourth) Amendment Act, 1971-Nature and scope of the amending power.

Article 13(2)-'Law' in 13(2) if includes amendment of the Constitution Distinction between legislative power and constituent power.

Article 368-"Amendment" meaning of-"Amendment" if includes the power to abrogate the Constitution-If includes the power to alter the basic structure or frame-work of the Constitution,

Fundamental Rights-If amendment can take away or abridge the rights guaranteed in Part III.

Fundamental Rights--If inalienable natur31 rights so as to operate as restriction on the amending power.

Implied and inherent limitations-Power of amendment if subject to inherent or implied limitations.

Preamble-Nature-Preamble, if operates as a source of implied limitation on the power of amendment.

Constitution (Twenty Fourth) Amendment Act 1971-Validity of-Amendment if enlargement of the limits of the Amending power.

Article 368-lf there are inherent or implied limitations in the article amended.

Constitution (Twenty Fifth) Amendment Act, 1971-Validity of. Section 2(a) & (b)-Substitution of 'amount' for 'compensation'-Exclusion of article 19(l)(f) to law in article 31(2) abrogates the basic structure of the Constitution-Meaning of 'amount'-Scope of judicial review of adequacy.

Section 3-lntroduction of new article 31C-Nature and object of the article if abrogates the essential features of the Constitution-If amounts to delegation of amending power to state legislatures-Effect of Declaration-Nexus of law under the article to the directives in article 39(b) and (c), if subjected to judicial review.

Directive Principles of State Policy-Importance in the constitutional scheme Relation with fundamental rights. Property, right to-Nature of the right.

Constitution (Twenty Ninth) Amendment Act, 1972-Validity of-Article 31B and 31A-lf interrelated.

Judicial Review-Limits of-Place of judicial review in the constitutional scheme.

Interpretation-Rules of Constitutional Interpretation-Constituent Assembly Debates, relevancy of.

The question whether the fundamental rights set out in Part III of the Constitution could be taken away or abridged by amendment of the Constitution was first considered by this Court in Sankari Prasad v. Union of India, [1952] S.C.R. 89. In Sankari Prasad the validity of the Constitution (First Amendment) Act 1951, was challenged. The First Amendment made changes in articles 15 and 19 of the Constitution and inserted articles 31A and 31B. The principal contention was that the First Amendment in so far as it purported to take away or abridge the rights conferred by Part _III of the Constitution fell within the prohibition of article 13(2) of the Constitution.

The Court unanimously held that the word 'law' in article 13(2) was relatable to exercise of ordinary legislative power and not amendments to the Constitution and that the terms of article 368 were general to empower Parliament to amend the Constitution without any exception. The question came up again in Sajjan singh v. State of Rajasthan, [1965] 1 S.C.R. 938, wherein the validity of the Constitution (Seventeenth Amendment) Act 1964, was challenged. The majority view in Sajjan Singh was that article 368 plainly and unambiguously meant amendment of all provisions of the Constitution and that the word 'law' in article 13(2) did not take in Constitution Amendments. Thereafter, in Golaknath v. State of Punjab, the Court, six against live, held that an amendment of the Constitution was 'law' within the meaning of article 13(2); therefore, if an amendment took away or abridged the fundamental rights it was void, that the Constitution First1 Fourth and Seventeenth Amendments abridged fundamental rights but were valid on the application of the doctrine of prospective overruling or acquiescence and that Parliament had no power from the date of the decision to amend any of the provisions of Part III so as to take away or abridge the fundamental rights.

One of the amendments affecting the right to property was the Constitution (Fourth Amendment) Act, 1955. The Amendment Act had enacted that no law providing for compulsory acquisition or requisitioning "shall be called in question in any Court on the ground that the compensation provided by that law is not adequate". The amendment was passed to get over the interpretation given by the Court in State of West Bengal v. Bela Baoerju, [1954] S.C.R. 674, to the word 'compensation' viz., just equivalent or full indemnification for the property expropriated. The effect of the amendment was considered by this Court in Vairavdu Mudaliar v. Deputy Collector, [1965] 1 S.C.R. 614. The Court took the view that the fact that Parliament used the same expressions, namely, 'compensation' and 'principles', as were found in article 31 before the amendment, was clear indication that Parliament accepted the meaning given by the Court to tho.9e expressions in Bela Banerjee's case. In Union of India v. Metal Corporation, [1967] 1 S.C.R. 255 the Court struck down the Metal Corporation (Acquisition of Undertaking) Act 1965, because the principles for determining the: compensation laid down in the Act did not represent the just equivalent of the property taken. Later, in State of Guiarat v. Shanti/ al Mangal Das, [1969] 3 S.C.R. 341, the Court overruled the decision in Metal Corporation case. The Court held that a challenge to a statute that the principles specified by it did not award a just equivalent would be in clear violation of the Constitutional declaration that adequacy of compensation provided was not justiciable, that just equivalent was not capable of precise determination by the application of any recognised principles and that "apart from the practical difficulties the law declared by this Court also placed serious obstacles in giving effect to the directive principles of State policy incorporated in article 39". Thereafter, in R. C. Cooper v. Union of India (The Bank Nationalisation Case) [1970] 3 S.C.R. 530 the Court by a majority, ten against one, held that even after the Fourth Amendment "Compensation" meant "the equivalent in terms of money of the property compulsorily acquired" "according to relevant principles which principles must be appropriate to the determination of compensation for the particular class of property sought to be acquired". Arguments were addressed mainly in Writ Petition No. 135 of 1970. In this Writ Petition the petitioner had challenged the validity of the Kerala Land Reforms Amendment Act 1969 and the Kerala Land Reforms Amendment Act, 1971, for the reason that some of the provisions thereof violated articles 14, 19(l)(f), 25, 26 and 31 of the Constitution. During the pendency of the Writ Petition Parliament passed_ three constitution amendments, namely the Constitution Twenty Fourth, Twenty Fifth and Twenty Ninth Amendment Acts. The Constitution Twenty Fourth Amendment Act amended article 368. It enacted that Parliament may, in exercise of its constituent power, amend by way of addition, variation or repeal any provision of the Constitution in accordance with the procedure laid down in that article. The other part of the amendment is that nothing in article 13 shall apply to any amendment under article 368°.

• Article 368 · before amendment.

Procedure for amendment of this Constitution: An amendment of Ibis Constitution may be initiated only by the introduction Of a Bill for the purpose in either House of Parliament. when the Bill is passed in each House by a majority Of the total membership of that House and by a majority of not less than two thirds of the members of that House present and voting, it shall be presented to President for his assent and upon such assent being given to the Bill the Constitution shall stand amended in accordance with the terms of the Bill. Provided that if such amendment seeks to make any change in:-

(a) article 54, article 55, article 73, article 162 or article 241; or

(b) Chapter IV of Part V. Chapter V of Pan VJ, or Chapter I of Part XI, or

(c) any of the Lists in the Seventh Schedule, or

(d) the representation of States in Parliament, or

(e) the provisions of this article, the amendment shall also require to be ratified by the Legislatures of not less than one-half of the States by resolution to that effect passed by those Legislatures before the Bill making provision for such amendment is presented to the President for absent. Article 368 after amendment-Article 368 of the Constitution shall be re-numbered as clause (2) thereof, and

(a) for the marginal heading of that article, the following marginal heading shall be substituted, namely :- " Power of Parliament to amend the Constitution and procedure therefore".

(b) before clause (2) as so re-numbered, the following clause shall be inserted, namely:- "Notwithstanding anything in this Constitution, Parliament may in exercise of its constitution Power amend by way of addition, variation or repeal any provision of this Constitution in accordance with the procedure laid down in this article".

(c) in clause (2) as so. re-numbered, for the words "it shall be presented to the President for his assent and upon such assent being given to the Bill", the words "if shall be presented to the President who shall give his assent to the Bill and thereupon" shall be substituted; (d) after clause (2) as so re-numbered, the following clause shall be inserted namely:-

(3) Nothing in Article 13 shall apply to any amendment made under this article.

The Constitution Twenty Fifth Amendment Amended article 31(2) and article 31(2-A). Section 2 of the Amendment Act substituted the word "amount" for the word "compensation" and excluded the application of article 19(1)(f) to a law under article 31(2). It was also made clear that no such law shall be called in question in any court on the ground that the whole or any port of such amount is to be given otherwise than in cash. Section 3 introduced new article 31C. It empowered Parliament and State Legislatures to enact law giving effect to the policy of the State towards securing the directive principles. in clause (b} or cl. (c) of article 39 and no such law could be questioned on the ground that it took away or abridged any of the rights conferred by articles 14, 19 and 31. Further, the amendment laid down that no law containing a declaration that it is for giving effect to such policy shall be called in question in any court on the ground that it does not give effect to such policy' . The provisions of the article were not to be applied to a law made by the Legislature of a state unless such law received the assent of the President. The Constitution (Twenty Ninth). Amendment Act included the Kerala and Reforms Acts in the Ninth Schedule to the Constitution making them immune from attack on the ground of violation of the fundamental rights. The Petitioner challenged the validity of the three Constitution Amendment Acts.

HELD : (By Full Court) : The Constitution (Twenty Fourth) amendment Act, Section 2(a) md 2(b) of the Constitution (Twenty Fifth) Amendment Act and the Constitution (Twenty Ninth) Amendment Act are valid.

By majority : As per Hegde, Ray, Jaganmohan Reddy, Palekar, Khanna, Mathew, Beg, Dwivedi, Mukherjee and Chandrachud, JI : The decision of the majority in Golaknath that the word "law" in article 13(2) included amendments to the Constitution and the article operated as a limitation upon the power to amend the Constitution in article 368 is erroneous and is overruled. By majority: Per Ray, Palekar, Khanna, Mathew, Beg, Dwivedi and Chandrachud, JJ : The power of amendment is plenary. It includes within itself the power to add, alter or repeal the various articles of the Constitution including those relating to fundamental rights.

By majority: Per Sikri, C.J. and Shelat, Hegde, Grover, Khanna, Jaganmohan Reddy and Mukherjea, JJ. (Ray, Palekar, Mathew, Beg, Dwivedi and Chandrachud, JJ. dissenting): The power to amend does not include the power to alter the basic structure or framework of the Constitution so as to change its identity.

By majority: Per Ray, Palekar, Khanna, Mathew, Beg, Dwivedi and Chandrachud JJ. (Sikri, C.J. and Shelat, Hegde, Grover, Mukherjee, JJ. holding contra and Jaganmohan Reddy, J. leaving the question open): The are no inherent or implied limitations on the power of amendment under article 368.

By majority: The first part of article 31C is valid. The second part of the article, viz., "and no law containing a declaration that it is for giving effect to such policy shall be called in question in any court on the ground that it does not give effect to such policy is invalid.

[Sikri, C.J. and Shelat, Hegde, Grove.r and Mukherjca, JJ. held both the parts of article 31C invalid. Ray, Palekar, Mathew, Beg, Dwivedi and Chandrachud, JJ. held both the parts of the article valid.

Jaganmohan Reddy J, held the second part of the article invalid and the first part of the article valid subject to the severance of the words "inconsistent with or takes away" and the words "article 14" therein.

• • •

CHAPTER II

MANEKA GANDHI Vs. UNION OF INDIA January 25, 1978

Citations: [1978] 2 SCR 621, (1978) 1 SCC 248

[M. H. BEG, C. J., Y. V. CHANDRACHUD, P. N. BHAGWATI, v. R. KRISHNA IYER, N. L. UNTWALIA, s. MURTAZA FAZAL ALI, AND P. S. KAILASAM, JJ.J

Constitution of India Articles 14, 19 (1) (a) and 11-Personal liberty Whether right to go abroad is part of personal liberty-Whether a law which ton1plies with Article 21 has still to meet the challenge of Article 19.-Nature and ambit of Article 14-ludging validity with reference to direct and inevitable effect-Whether the right under Article 19(1) (a) has any geographical limitation.

Passports Act, 1967-Ss. 3,5,6,10(3)(c), 10(5)-Whether s.10(3)(c)_is violative of Articles 14, 19(1) (a) (b) & 21-Grounds for refusing to grant passport-Whether the power to impound passport arbitrary-"in general public interest" if vague.

Principles of Natural Justice-Whether applies only to quasi judicial orders D or applies 10 administrative orders affecting rights of citizens-When statute silent whether can be implied-Duty to act judicially whether can be spelt out -- ln urgent cases whether principles of natural justice can apply.

The petitioner was issued a passport on June 1, 1976 under the Passport Act, 1967. On the 4th of July 1977, the petitioner received a letter dated 2nd July, 1977, from the Regional Passport Officer Delhi intimating to her that it was decided by the Government of India to impound her passport under s. 10(3)(c) E of the Act "in public interest". The petitioner was required to surrender her passport within 7 days from the receipt of that letter. The petitioner immediately addressed a letter to the Regional Passport Officer requesting him to furnish a copy of the statement of reasons for making the order as provided in s.10(5). A reply was sent by the Government of India, Ministry of External Affairs on 6th July 1977 stating inter alia that the Government decided "in the interest of the general public" not to furnish her copy of the statement of reasons for the making of the order. The petitioner thereupon filed the present Writ Petition challenging action of the Government in impounding her passport and declining F to give reasons for doing so. The Act was enacted on 24-4-67 in view of the decision of this Court in Satwant Singh Sawliney's case. The position which obtained prior to the coming into force of the Act was that there was no law regulating the issue of passports for leaving the shores of India and going abroad. The issue of passport was entirely within the unguided and unchallenged discretion: of the Executive. In Satwant Singh's, case, this Court held by a majority that the expression 'personal liberty' in Article 21 takes in, the right of locomotion and travel abroad and under Art. 21 no person can be deprived of his right to go abroad except according to the procedure established by law. This decision was accepted by the Parliament and the infirmity pointed out by it was set right by the enactment of the Passports Act, 1967. The preamble of the Act shows that it was enacted to provide for the issue of passport and travel documents to regulate the departure from India of citizens of India and other persons and for incidental and ancillary matters. Section 3 provides that no person shall depart from or attempt to depart from India unless he holds in this behalf a valid passport or travel document. Section 5(1) provides for making of an application for issue of a passport or travel document for visiting foreign country. Sub-section (2) of section 5 says that on receipt of such application the Passport Authority, after making such enquiry, if any, as it may consider necessary shall, by order in writing, issue or refuse to issue the passport or travel document or make or refuse to make that passport or travel document endorsement in respect of one or more of the foreign countries specified in the application. Sub-section (3) requires the Passport Authority where it refuses to issue the passport or travel document or to make any endorsement to record in writing a brief statement of its reasons for n1aking such order. Section 6(1) lays down the grounds on which the Passport Authority shall refuse to make an endorsement for visiting any foreign country and provides that on no other ground the endorsement shall be refused. Section 6 (2) specifies the grounds on which alone and on no other grounds the Passport Authority shall refuse to issue the Passport 01 travel document for visiting any foreign country and amongst various ground~ set out there the last is that in the opinion of the Central Government the issue of passport or travel document to the applicant will not be in the public interest Sub-section (1) of section 10 empowers the Passport Authority to vary or can· eel the endorsement on a passport or travel document or to vary or cancel it or the conditions subject to which a passport or travel document has been issue having regard to, inter alia,. The provisions of s. 6(1) or any notification under · s. 19. Sub-section (2) confers powers on the Passport Authority to vary o: cancel the conditions of the passport or travel document on the application o: the holder of the passport or travel document and with the previous approvaI of the Central Government. Sub-section (3) provides that the Passport Authority may impound or cause to be impounded or revoke a passport or travel document on the grounds set out in cl. (a) to (h). The order impounding the passport in the present, case, was made by the Central Government under cl. (c) which reads as follows :-

" (c) lf the passport authority deems it necessary so to do in the interest of the sovereignty and integrity of India, the security of India, friendly relations of India with the foreign country, or in the interests of the general public."

Sub-section (5) requires the Passport Authority impounding or revoking a passport or travel document or varying or cancelling an endorsement made upon it to record in writing a brief statement of the reasons for making such order ar d furnish to the holder of the passport or travel document on demand a copy l)f the same. unless, in any case, the Passport Authority is of the opinion that it will not be in the interest of the sovereignty and integrity of India, the security of India, friendly relations of lndia with any foreign country, or in the interest of the general public to furnish such a copy. The Central Government declined to furnish a copy of this statement of reasons for impounding the passport of t 1e petitioner on the ground that it was not in the interest of the general public to furnish such copy to the petitioner.

The petitioner contended.

- The right to go abroad is part of "personal liberty" within the meaning of that expression as used in Art. 21 and no one can be deprived of this right except according to the procedure prescribed by law. There is no procedure prescribed by the Passport Act, for impounding or revoking a Passport. Even if some procedure can be traced in the said Act it is unreasonable and arbitrary in as much as it does not provide for giving an opportunity to the holder of be Passport to be heard against the making of the order.
- Section 10(3) (c) is violative of fundamental rights guaranteed under Articles 14, 19(1) (a) and (g) and 21.

- The impugned order is made in contravention of the rules of natural justice and is, therefore, null and void. The impugned order has effect of placing an unreasonable restriction on the right of free speech and expression guaranteed to the petitioner under Article 19(1) (a) as also on the right to carry on the profession of a journalist conferred under Art. 19(1) (g).
- The impugned order could not consistently with Articles 19(1)(a.) and (g) be passed on a mere information of the Central Government that the presence of the· petitioner is likely to be required in connection with the proceedings before the Commission of Inquiry.
- In order that a passport may be impounded under s. 10(3)(c), public interest must actually exist in present and mere likelihood of public interest arising in future would be no ground for impounding the passport.
- It was not correct to say that the petitioner was likely to be required for giving evidence before the Shah Commission.

The respondents denied the contentions raised by the petitioner.
BEG, C. J., (Concurring with Bhagwati, J.)

• • •

CHAPTER III

MINERVA MILLS LTD. & ORS, Vs. UNION OF INDIA & ORS. July 31, 1980

Citations: [1981] 1 SCR 206, (1980) 3 SCC 625

[Y. V. CHANDRACHUD, C. J., P. N. BHAGWATI, A. c. GUPTA, N. LUNTWALIA AND P. S. KAILASAM, JJ.] Constitution of India Forty Second Amendment Act, Sections 4 and 55- Whether the Sections are beyond the amending power of the Parliament under Article 368 of the Constitution and therefore void-Whether the Directive Principles of State policy contained in Part iv of the Constitution can have primacy over the fundamental rights conferred by Part III of the Constitution-Constitution of India Articles 14, 19, 31C, 38 and 368.

Minerva Mills Ltd. is a limited company dealing in textiles. On August 20, 1970 the Central Government appointed a committee under section 15 of the Industries (Development Regulation) Act, 1951' to make a full and complete-- investigation of the affairs of the Minerva Mills Ltd. as it was of the opinion that there had been or was likely to be substantial fall in the volume of production. The said Committee submitted its report to the Central Government in January 1971, on the basis of which the Central Government passed an order dated October 19, 1971 under section 18A of the 1951' Act, authorising the National Textile Corporation Ltd., to take over the management of the Mills on the ground that its affairs are being managed iii a· manner highly detrimental to public interest. This undertaking was nationalised and taken over by the Central Government under the provisions of the Sick Textile Undertakings (Nationalisation) Act, 1974'. The petitioners challenged the constitutional validity of certain provisions of the· Sick Textile Undertakings (Nationalisation) Act, 1974 and of the order dated October 19, 1971, the constitutionality-- of the Constitution (Thirty Ninth Amendment) Act which inserted the impugned Nationalisation Act as Entry 105 in. the Ninth Schedule to the Constitution, the validity of Article 31B of the Constitution and finally the constitutionality-- of sections 4 and 55 of the Constitution (Forty Second Amendment) Act, 1976. on the ratio of the majority judgment in Kesavananda Bharati's case, namely, though by Article 368 of the Constitution Parliament is given the power to· amend the Constitution, that power cannot be exercised SQ as to damage the basic features of the Constitution or so as to destroy its basic structure.

Opining that sections 4 and 55 of the Constitution (Forty Second Amendment) Act are void and beyond the amending power of the Parliament the· Court by majority (Per Chandrachud. C.J . on behalf of himself, A. C. Gupta. N. L. Untwalia & P. S. Kailasam, JJ.)·

• • •

CHAPTER IV

SHARAD BIRDHI CHAND SARDA Vs. STATE OF MAHARASHTRA July 17, 1984

Citations: [1985] 1 SCR 88, (1984) 4 SCC 116

(S. MURTAZA FAZAL ALI, A. VARADARAJAN AND SABYASACH! MUKHARJI, JJ.J

Constitution of India, 1950, Article 136-lnterference by the Supre1ne Court with the concurrent findings of fact of the courts below, normally not permissible Special circumstance like errors of law, violation of well-established principles of criminal jurisprudence etc. would be necessary for interference.

Evidence-Circumstantial evidence, nature and proof of -Conditions precedent for conviction-Evidence Act Section 3 (Act 1 of 1972).

Evidence-Circu1nstantia/ evidence-Onus of proof-Prosecution must prove every link of the chain and complete chain-Infirmity or lacuna in the prosecution cannot be cured by false defence or plea-A person cannot be convicted on pure 1noral conviction-False explanation can be used as additional link to fortify the prosecution case, subject to satisfaction of certain conditions.

Doctrine of Proximity, concept of, nature and limits explained-Admissibility of statements and dying declarations under sections 8, 32 of the Evidence Act.

Murder by administration of poison-Circumstances that should be looked into before a conviction-Penal Code (Act XLV of 1860) Section 300.

Evidence, appreciation of-Evidence of interested witnesses, especially that of close relatives of the deceased-Duty of the Court-Evidence Act (Act I of 1872) Section 3.

Benefit of doubt-When two views are ·possible, one leading to the guilt of the accused and the other leading to his innocence, the benefit of doubt should go to the accused entitling his acquittal-Evidence Act (Act I of 1872) Sections JOI -104

Examination of the accused under Section 313 of Crl. P.C.-Circumstances not put to the accused to explain, cannot be considered for conviction-Code of Crin1inal Procedure, 1973 (Act II of 1974) Section 313.

The appellant, Ran1eshwar, Birdhichand Sarda, ·Ramvilas Rambagas Sarda, were accused 1, 2 and 3 respectively in Sessions Case No. 203 of 1982 on the file of the Additional Sessions Judge, Pune. The appellant and the second accused are the sons of one Birdhichand of Pune whose family has a cloth business. In addition, the appellant, a graduate in Chemical Engineering had started a chemical factory at Bhosari, a suburb of Pune. The third accused is uncle of the appellant and· the second accused. The appellant is the husband of Manjushree alias Manju while the second accused is the husband of Anuradha (P.W, 35). Birdhichand's family has its residential house at Ravivar Peth in Pune and owns a flat in a building known as Takshasheela Apartments in Mukund Nagar area of Pune. All the three accused were charged for the alleged offence of murder by poisoning on the night of 11/12.6,1982 of Manju the newly married wife of the first accused and the appellant herein under section B 302 J.P.C. read with section.1208. Accused No. 3was also charged under section 201 read with Section 120B I.P.C. The whole case vested on the circumstantial evidence based on certain letters alleged to have been written by the deceased to some of the witnesses and other statements of the deceased to them and the medical report. On an appreciation of the evidence the trial court found all the three accused guilty as charged, convicted them accordingly and ·sentenced the appellant to death under s.302 I.P.C. and all the three accused to rigorous imprisonn1ent for two years and a fine of Rs. 2,000 each under s.120B I.P.C. but did not award any sentence under s.201 read with s.120B.

The appellant and the other two accused file Criminal Appeal No. 265/ 83 against their conviction and the sentences awarded to them. The State filed a Criminal Revision application for enhance1nent of the sentence awarded to accused 2 and 3. The appeal as well as Criminal Revision application was heard along with confirmation case No. 3 of 1983 together by the Division Bench of the Bombay High Court which allowed the appellants appeal in part regarding_ his conviction and sentence under s.120B I.P.C. but confirmed his conviction and sentence of death awarded under section 302 I.P.C., allowed the appeal of accused 2 and 3 in full and acquitted them and dismissed the Crin1inal Revision Application. Hence the appellant alone has come up before the Supreme Court after obtaining Special Leave.

Allowing the appeal, the Court.

HELD: (Per Fazal Ali, J.).

1:1. Normally, the Supreme Court does not interfere with the concurrent findings of the fact of the courts below. in the absence of very special circumstances or gross errors of law committed by the High Court. But, where the High Court ignores or overlooks the crying circumstance and proved facts, or violates and misapplies the well-established principles of criminal jurisprudence or decision rendered by this Court on appreciation of circumstantial evidence and refuses to give benefit of doubt to the accused despite facts apparent on the face of the record or on its own finding or tries to gl9ss over them without giving any reasonable explanation or commits errors of G law apparent on the face of the record which results in serious and substantial miscarriage of justice to the accused, it is the duty of this Court to step in and correct the legally erroneous decision of the High Court. (174E-G)

1 :2. Suspicion, however, great it may be, cannot take the place of legal proof. A moral conviction however, strong or genuine cannot amount to a legal conviction supportable in law. [174Hl

1:3. The well-established rule of criminal justice is 'fouler the crime higher the proof'. In the instant case, the life and liberty of a subject was at stake. As the accused was given a capital sentence a very careful cautious and meticulous approach necessarily had to be made by the Court. [175AJ

2:1. The Indian law on the question of the nature and scope of dying declaration has made a distinct departure from the English Jaw where only the statement which directly relate to the cause of death are admissible. The second part of cl.(1) of s.32, viz, "the circumstances of the transaction which resulted in his death, in cases in which the cause of that person's death comes into question" is not to be found in the English Law. [l07FwG

2:2. From a review of the various authorities of the Courts and the clear language of s.32(1) of Evidence Act, the following propositions emerge: [108F]

(l) Section 32 is an exception to the rule of hearsay and makes admissible the statement of a person who dies. whether the death is a homicide or a suicide, provided the statement relates to the cause of death, or relates to circumstances leading to the death. In this respect, Indian Evidence Act, in view of the peculiar conditions of our society and the diverse nature and character of our people, has thought it necessary to widen the sphere of s.32 to avoid injustice. [1080-H]

(2) The test of proximity cannot be too literally construed and practically reduced to a cut-and-dried formula of universal application so

as to be confined in a straitjacket. Distance of time would depend or very with the circumstances of each case. For instance, where death is a logical culmination of a continuous drama long in process and is, as it were, a finale of the story, the statement regarding each step directly connected with the end of the drama would be admissible because the entire statement would have to be read as on organic whole and not torn from‘ the context. Sometimes statements relevant to or furnishing an immediate motive may also be admissible as being a part of the transaction of death. It is manifest that all these statements come to light only after the death of the deceased who speaks from death. For instance, where the death takes place within a very short time of the marriage or the distance of time is not spread over more than 3-4 months the statements may be admissible under s.32. [109B·Dl

(2) The test of proximity cannot be too literally construed and practically reduced to a cut-and-dried formula of universal application so as to be confined in a straitjacket .. Distance of time would depend or very with the circumstances of each case. For instance, where death is a logical culmination of a continuous drama long in process and is, as it were, a finale of the story, the statement regarding each step directly connected with the end of the drama would be admissible because the entire statement would have to be read as on organic whole and not torn from’ the context. Sometimes statements relevant to or furnishing an immediate motive may also be admissible as being a part of the transaction of death. It is manifest that all these statements come to light only after the death of the deceased who speaks from death. For instance, where the death takes place within a very short time of the marriage or the distance of time is not spread over more than 3-4 months the statements may be admissible under s.32. [109B·Dl

(3) The second part of cl.1 of s.32 is yet another exception to the rule that in criminal law the evidence of a person who was not being subjected to or given an opportunity of being cross-examined by the accused, would be valueless because the place of cross-examination is taken by the solemnity and sanctity of oath for the simple reason that a person on the verge of death is'" not likely to make a false statement unless there is strong evidence to show that G the statement was secured either by prompting or tutoring, [109E·F]

(4) Section 32 does not speak of homicide alone but includes suicide also, hence all the circumstance which may be relevant to prove a case of

homicide would be equally relevant to prove a case of suicide. [109-CJ-]

(5) Where the main evidence consists of statements and letters written by the deceased which are directly connected with or related to her death and which reveal a tell-tale story, the said "statement would clearly fell within the· four corners of s.32 and, therefore, admissible. The distance of time alone in-- A such cases would not make the statement irrelevant. [l09H]

• • •

CHAPTER V

A.R. ANTULAY Vs. R.S. NAYAK & ANR. APRIL 29, 1988

Citations: [1988] 1 Suppl. SCR 1, (1988) 2 SCC 602

[SABYASACHI MUKHARJI, RANGANATH MISRA, G.L. OZA, B.C. RAY, S. NATARAJAN, M.N. VENKATACHALIAH AND S. RANGANATHAN, JJ.]

Constitution of India, 1950: Articles 13, 14, 21, 32 Prosecution of appellant for offences under sections 161 and 165 I. P. C.-Trial under Criminal Law Amendment Act, 1952 to be held by Special Judge only- C Supreme Court in its judgment directing trial to be held by High Court Judge-Validity of Supreme Court Judgment-Whether infringement of fundamental right of accused involved-Whether procedure established by law violated-Power to create or enlarge jurisdiction-Legislative in character.

Articles 32, 134, 136, 137, 139, 141 and 142-Powers of review-. Nature and scope of-Whether Supreme Court can review its directions if they result in deprivation of fundamental rights of a citizen-Whether Supreme Court can issue writ of certiorari to quash judicial order passed by another Bench-Whether a larger Bench can overrule or recall a decision of a smaller Bench.

Articles 140, 141, 142 and 145: Jurisdiction-Want of-Can be established only by a superior court-No decision can be impeached collaterally by any inferior court-Superior court can always correct errors by petition or ex debito justitiae-Judgments per incuriam-Effect of.

Criminal Law (Amendment) Act, 1952: Sections 6 & 7- 0ffences under Act to be tried only by Special Judge-Order of Supreme Court transferring and directing trial by High Court Judge Whether legally authorised-Non-substance clause ins. 7(1)-Effect of.

Criminal Procedure Code, 1973: Sections 374, 406 & 407- Transfer of case-Power of transfer postulates that Court to which transfer or withdrawal is sought is competent to exercise jurisdiction over case-Intra state transfer is within jurisdiction of the appropriate D E F G High Court.

Practice and Procedure: Judgment of Supreme Court-Directions issued in proceedings inter parties-Found bad in law or violative of Articles 14 and 21 of the Constitution and principles of natural justice-Whether immune from correction even though they cause prejudice and do injury.

Criminal Trial-Criminal Procedure Code, 1973-Sec. 223- Whether an accused can demand as of a right trial with co-accused.

Interpretation of statutes-Words to be given normal meaning with reference to context-Golden rule of interpretation-When to be resorted to.

Legal Maxims: Actus curiae neminem gravabid-Coram nonjudice-Per curiam-Ex debito justitiae-Nunc-Pro-tunc-Applicability of.

The appellant was the Chief Minister of Maharashtra between June 9, 1980 and January 12, 1982, when he resigned that office in deference to the judgment of High Court in a writ petition filed against him, but continued as an MLA.

On August 9, 1982, respondent No. 1, a member of a political party tiled a complaint before a Special Judge against the appellant and others for offences under ss. 161 and 165 of the Indian Penal Code and s. 5 of the Criminal Law Amendment Act, 1952 and also under ss. 384 and 420 read with ss. 109 and 120B of the Indian Penal Code.

The Special Judge issued process to the appellant. Later, the Special Judge over-ruled the objection of the appellant to take cognizance of the offences on a private complaint, and to issue process, in the absence of notification under s. 7(2) of the Criminal Law Amendment Act, 1952, specifying as to which of the three special Judges of the area should try such cases.

Against this, the appellant filed a revision application in the High Court, which dismissed it subsequently. The appellant's Special Leave Petition against this was dismissed by the Supreme Court which held that the complaint filed by respondent No. 1 was clearly maintainable and cognizance was properly taken of it.

During the pendency of the revision application in the High Court, the State Government notified the Special Judge to try the offences specified under s. 6(1) of the Act and appointed another Special Judge, who discharged the appellant, holding that a member of the Legislative Assembly was a public servant and there was no valid sanction for prosecuting the appellant. Against this order of discharge, respondent No. 1 filed a Criminal Revision Application in the High Court, which was subsequently withdrawn to this Court.

On an appeal filed by respondent No. 1 directly under Article 136 • of the Constitution against the order of discharge, the Supreme Court held on 16.2.1984, that a member of the Legislative Assembly was not -,1. a public servant, and set aside the order of the Special Judge. The Court observed that though nearly 2'/z years had rolled by since prosecution against the accused, who was Chief Minister of a State, was launched and his character and integrity came under cloud, the case had not moved an inch further and that an expeditious trial was primarily in the interest of the accused and mandate of Article 21. It further observed that expeditious disposal of a criminal case was in the interest of both the prosecution and the accused. It, therefore, suo motu withdrew this special case and another one filed against the appellant by another person and transferred them to the High Court, with the request to the Chief Justice to assign these two cases to a sitting Judge of the High Court, who should proceed to expeditiously dispose of the cases, preferably by holding trial from day to day.

Pursuant to the directions of this Court dated February 16, 1984 the Chief Justice of the High Court assigned the cases to one of the Judges of that Court. The appellant appeared before him and raised an objection that the case could be tried only by a Special Judge appointed by the Government under the 1952 Act. The Judge rejected this and other objections holding that he was bound by the order of the Supreme Court.

Special. Leave Petitions as well as a writ petition filed by the appellant against the aforesaid decision were dismissed by this Court on April 17, 1984, holding that the Judge was perfectly justified, and indeed it was his duty to follow the decision of this Court which was binding on him. It also observed that the writ petition challenging the validity of the order and judgment of this Court as nullity or otherwise could not be entertained, and that the dismissal of the writ petition would not prejudice the petitioner's right to approach this Court, with an appropriate review petition or any other application, which he may be entitled to, in law.

Thereafter, the cases were transferred to another Special Judge, who framed 21 charges and declined to frame 22 other charges proposed by respondent No. 1. This Court allowed respondent No. I's appeal by special leave except in regard to three draft charges under s. 384 IPC, and requested the High Court to nominate another Judge to try the cases.

The Judge, to whom the cases were transferred, framed 79 charges against the appellant, and refused to proceed against the other named conspirators.

Against the aforesaid order, the appellant filed a Special Leave Petition before this Court questioning the jurisdiction of the Special Judge to try the case in violation of the appellant's fundamental rights ·conferred by Articles 14 and 21 and the provisions of the Criminal Law Amendment

Act of 1952. The appellant also filed a Special Leave Petition against the decision of the Judge, holding that none of the 79 charges framed against the accused required sanction under s. 197(1) of the Cr. P.C., and a writ petition challenging a portion of s. 197(1) as ultra vires Articles 14 and 21 of the Constitution.

This Court granted special leave in the Special Leave Petition questioning the jurisdiction of the Special Judge to try the case and stayed further proceedings in the High Court. It also issued notice in the other Special Leave Petition and the writ petition, and directed these to be tagged on to the appeal.

An application filed by respondent No. I for revocation of the Special Leave was dismissed and the appeal was referred to a Bench of seven Judges. The other Special Leave Petition and the writ petition were delinked, to be heard after the disposal of the appeal.

In the appeal, two questions arose, namely, (1) whether the directions given by this Court on 16th February, 1984, withdrawing the special cases pending in the Court of Special Judge and transferring the same to the High Court with the request to the Chief Justice to assign these cases to a sitting Judge of that High Court in breach of s. 7(1) of the Criminal Law Amendment Act, 1952 which mandated that the offences, as in this case, should be tried only by a Special Judge, thereby denying at least one right of appeal to the appellant was violative of Articles 14 and 21 of the Constitution and whether such directions were not at all valid or legal and (2) if such directions were not at all valid or legal in view of the Court's order of April 17, 1984, whether the present appeal was sustainable or the grounds therein justiciable in these proceedings. In other words, whether the said directions in a proceeding inter parties were binding even if bad in law or violative of Articles 14 and 21 of the Constitution and as such, immune from correction by this Court even though they caused prejudice and injury.

Allowing the appeal, and setting aside and quashing all the proceedings subsequent to the directions of the Court on 16.2.1984 and directing that the trial should proceed in accordance with law, i.e. Criminal Law Amendment Act, 1952.

HELD:

Majority: Sabyasachi Mukharji, Oza and Natarajan, JJ. Per Sabyasachi Mukharji, J:

I. Section 7(1) of the · Criminal Law Amendment Act, 1952 creates a condition which is sine qua non for the trial of offences under s. 6(1) of the said Act. The condition is that notwithstanding anything contained in the Code of Criminal Procedure or any other law, the said offences shall be triable by Special Judges only. The offences specified under s. 6(1) of the 1952 Act are those punishable under ss. 161, 162, 163, 164 and 165A of the Indian Penal Code and s. 5 of the Prevention of CorruptionAct,1947. [44B-C,49H, A]

• • •

CHAPTER VI

KIHOTO HOLLOHAN Vs. ZACHILLHU AND OTHERS NOVEMBER 12, 1991/FEB. 18, 1992

Citations: [1992] 1 SCR 686, (1992) Supp 2 SCC 651

[LALIT MOHAN SHARMA, M.N. VENKATACHALIAH, J.S. VERMA K. JAYACHANDRA REDDY AND S.C. AGRAWAL, JJ.]

Constitution - validity of amendment - Constitution (52nd Amendment) Act, 1985 - petition challenging insertion of 10th schedule to Constitution - para 7 of 10 Schedule which brings about change in operation of Articles 136, 226 and 227 made without ratification of State Legislature as provided under Article 368 (2) invalid - non observance of such condition precedent does not affect severability of Para 7 from other parts of amendment - 52nd amendment excluding para 7 valid - para 2 of 10th Schedule neither violate democratic rights of elected members nor freedom of speech and freedom of vote and conscience - Para 2 is not violative of Articles 105 and 194 - Speakers/Chairmen under 10th Schedule exercise power of Tribunal to adjudicate rights and obligations of elected members and their decisions amenable to judicial review - judicial review does not cover any stage prior to making decisions by Presiding Officers - interlocutory interference can be made when interlocutory disqualifications or suspension may have grave, immediate and irreversible repercussion and consequence - concept of statutory finality of decisions of Presiding Officers in Para 6 (2) does not affect right of judicial review under Articles 136, 226 and 227 based on violation of constitutional mandates, mala fides, non-compliance with Rules of natural justice and perversity - deeming provision in Para 6 (2) would attract immunity analogous to that of Articles 122 (1) and 212 (1) as explained in Kesav Singh's case.

ORDER;

The Transfer Petition is allowed and the Writ Petition, Rule No. 2421 of 1990 on the file of the High Court of Guwahati is withdrawn to this Court for the purpose of deciding the constitutional issues and of declaring the law on the matter.

In accordance with the majority opinion, the factual controversies raised in the Writ Petition will, however, have to be decided by the High Court Applying the principles declared and laid down by the majority. The Writ

Petition is, accordingly remitted to the High Court for such disposal in accordance with law.

1. In these petitions the constitutional validity of the Tenth Schedule of the Constitution introduced by the Constitution (Fifty-Second Amendment) Act, 1985, is assailed. These two cases were amongst a batch of Writ Petitions, Transfer Petitions, civil Appeals, Special Leave Petitions and other similar and connected matters raising common questions which were all heard together. On 12.11.1991 we made an order pronouncing our findings and conclusions upholding the constitutional validity of the amendment and of the provisions of the Tenth Schedule, except for Paragraph 7 which was declared invalid for want of ratification in terms of and as required by the proviso to Article 368 (2) of the Constitution. In the order dated 12.11.1991 our conclusions were set out and we indicated that the reasons for the conclusions would follow later. The reasons for the conclusions are now set out.

2. This order is made in Transfer Petition No. 40 of 1991 and in Writ Petition No. 17 of 1991. We have not gone into the factual controversies raised in the Writ-Petition before the Writ-Petition before the Guwahati High Court in Rule No. 2421 of 1990 from which Transfer Petition No. 40 of 1991 arises. Indeed, in the order of 12th November, 1991 itself the said Writ Petition was remitted to the High Court for its disposal in accordance with law.

We have reached the conclusion that para 7 of the Tenth Schedule is unconstitutional; that the entire Tenth Schedule is constitutionally invalid in the absence of prior ratification in accordance with the proviso to Clause (2) of Article 368; that the Doctrine of Severability does not apply in the present case of a constitutional amendment which suffers from the defect of absence of ratification as required by the proviso to Clause (2) of Article 368; that the remaining part of the Tenth Schedule minus para 7 is also unconstitutional for violation of a basic feature of the Constitution; and that the entire Tenth Schedule is, therefore, constitutionally invalid rendering the Constitution (Fifty-Second Amendment) Act, 1985 still born and an abortive attempt to amend the constitution. In view of this conclusion, it is not necessary for us to express our concluded opinion on the other grounds of challenge to the constitutional validity of the entire Tenth Schedule urged at the hearing on the basis of alleged violation of certain other basic features of the Constitution including the right of members based on Article 105 of the Constitution.

• • •

CHAPTER VII

INDRA SAWHNEY VS. UNION OF INDIA, NOVEMBER 16, 1992

Citations: [1992] 2 Suppl. SCR 454, 1992 Supp (3) SCC 217

Ranganath Misra, Acting C.J., K.N. Singh, M.H. Kania, Kuldip Singh and P.B. Sawant, JJ.

Constitution - backward class - Order passed on recommendations of mandal commission - many violent incidents took place after Order was made - legitimate interest of every backward class to be protected - identification of castes continues but no further steps to implement this Order shall be taken.

Held,

1. Three out of us sitting as a Bench on the 21st September, 1990, made an order after hearing parties where we had indicated that the decision to implement three aspects of the recommendations of the Mandal Commission was a political one and ordinarily the Court would not interfere with such a decision.

2. This is what we had said there "lot of emphasis has been laid on either side on the human factor. It was particularly brought to our notice that subsequent to the order of 11th September, 1990, agitation has spread into every nook and corner of the country and public life has been disturbed; human lives have been lost and Government property has been damaged and destroyed. While we lake notice of it, we are of the view that there is no particular necessity for judicial interference on that sole ground."

3. Thereafter, we had made an appeal to the entire nation that the matter was being adjudicated by this Court and everybody's rights would be worked out when the matter is heard and nothing shall impede this Court from working out the rights of parties and giving such relief as is ultimately adjudicated to be due.

4. This petition on behalf of the Supreme Court Bar Association has been brought up by highlighting incidents which have taken place after that order was made.

5. We have heard learned Counsel on either side at considerable length. We have also listened to interveners and parties in person.

6. The learned Attorney General had told us on the earlier occasion that identification of castes would take about two to three months. It is not in dispute that until such identification is made no further steps for conferring benefits contained in the Government's order dated 13th August, 1990 can at all be worked out.

7. At the request of counsel for all the parties we propone the hearing of the matters from 6.1.1.1990 to 25.10.1990. We are of the view that till the end of November there would be no occasion for proceeding with the implementation of the Government Order excepting identification of the castes to be benefited.

8. In fact the real implication of the order of 21.9.1990 was that there was nothing going to happen before the matter was heard by this Court. We would, however, reiterate without taking into consideration the submissions with reference to the happenings after the 21st September that the identification of the castes shall continue but until the matter is heard and we expect it to be finished before the end of the year - no further steps should be taken. No other steps to implement the order of 13.8.1990 shall be taken.

9. The earlier order relating to recruitment of doctors by U.P.S.C. is left unaffected as the question of reservation shall not arise until after the written examination.

10. We make it clear that we expect that law and order situation shall immediately improve, both parties shall take our appeal seriously and restore peace so that the hearing of the matter can be taken up by this Court in an appropriate atmosphere.

11. We reiterate that the legitimate interest of every backward class shall be appropriately protected. We make it further clear that the order made today is only a clarification of the order made on 21st September, 1990 bringing out the real purport.

12. Learned Attorney General in course of his submissions has clarified that prevailing benefits of reservation for the handicapped have not been affected by the Government Order.

13. All the interlocutory applications for intervention filed till today shall be accepted by the Registry.

14. List the matters on 25.10.1990.

15. The full text of our order shall be immediately released to the Press and the Government controlled media for the purpose of transmission to the public at large.

• • •

CHAPTER VIII

S.R. BOMMAI AND ORS. Vs. UNION OF INDIA AND ORS. MARCH 11, 1994

Citations: [1994] 2 SCR 644, (1994) 3 SCC 1

[S. RATNAVEL PANDIAN; A. M. AHMADI, KULDIP SINGH, J.S. VERMA, P.B. SAWANT, K. RAMASWAMY, S.C. AGRAWAL, YOGESHWAR DAYAL AND B.P. JEEVAN REDDY, J.T.]

Constitution of India, I950: Art. 356-Nature, scope, applicability and effect of-President's Rule-Promulgation of in case of failure of constitutional machinery in states-Satisfaction of President that a situation has arisen in which the Government of the State cannot be carried on in accordance with the provisions of the Constitution-interpretation of-Satisfaction of President-'Satisfaction'-Meaning of-Subjective satisfaction of Union D Council of Ministers-Principles of natural justice-Observance of-Satisfaction must be based on Objective material-Situations where it can be said that the State Govt. 'cannot' be carried on-Return of any political party at the centre different from that in power in the State-Not one such situation-ideology of State Govt. to be consistent with the Constitution-Disregard IE by any State of the basic values and essential features of the Constitution-Regard to federal structure and Centre State relation-Need for-Effect of issuance of the Promulgation and conditions precedent-Dissolution of Legislative Assembly and Government of the State-.Whether a necessary consequence-Effect of approval/disapproval of the Promulgation-Revival of Legislation Assembly-Validation of laws and orders passed during the ~ promulgation-Validity of Promulgations issued in respect of Karnataka, Meghalaya, Nagaland, Madhya Pradesh, Himachal Pradesh and Rajasthan. precedent-Dissolution of Legislative Assembly and Government of the State-Whether a necessary consequence-Effect of approval/disapproval of the Promulgation-Revival of Legislation Assembly-Validation of laws and orders passed during the ~ promulgation-Validity of Promulgations issued in respect of Karnataka, Meghalaya, Nagaland, Madhya Pradesh, Himachal Pradesh and Rajasthan.

Constitution of India, I950-Arts. 356, and 352, 355, 357, 36o-Nature of Art. 356 in the context of-An emeJ8ency provision to be used in exceptional circumstances.

Constitution of India, 1950-Arts. 356(1) and 154, 155, 156, 163-'On receipt of report from Governor'-Governor's obligation to make report-Role of Governors-Floor test-Testing majority support of the ruling party in the State on the floor of the House-Necessity of-Whether floor test a pre-requisite to sending report by Governor.

Constitution of India, 1950-Preamble and Arts. 15, 16, 25, 26, 27, 28, A 30, 51-A, 356-Scope of Preamble &-Secularism-Meaning and role of-Religious tolerance and equal treatment of all religions-Concept of positive secularism-Religion vis-a-vis secularism-Secularism is part of the basic structure of the Constitution-Effect of 42nd Amendment.

Constitution of India 1950-Arts. 32, 226 & 35-Proclamation under Art.356-Amenable to judicial review-Before or after Parliament's approval-Not the subjective satisfaction of President but material on which satisfaction is based open to judicial review on grounds of illegality, malafide, extraneous considerations, abuse of power or fraud on power, irrelevance not sustainable so long as there is some relevant material-Corrections or adequacy of the material cannot be gone into on merits-Nor can purely political questions be reviewed by Court-Doctrine of political thicket-Materials falling within the expression, 'or otherwise'-Review of.

Constitution of India, 1950-Arts. 356, 74(2) & 142 and 32 & 226-Proclanmation under Art. 356-Judicial Review.-Bar under Art. 74(2)-Nature and object of-Whether confined to the advice tendered by Council of Ministers-But material on the basis of which advice was tendered is subject to judicial review-Whether Govt. while justifying its action can claim privilege under S. 123 of the Evidence Act, 187l-Burden of Proof-First on the person challenging the Proclamation-Then shifts to Union of India.

Constitution of India: Arts. 74 and 77-Scope of Interpretation of the Constitution: Constitutional scheme &-Should be so construed as to maintain the fundamental balance.

Constitutional provisions-Language plain and clean-No obvious in advertento: mission-Filling up the gaps by Courts-Whether could be resorted to.

Constitutional provisions-Interpretation not to whittle down the powers of the States. Evidence Act, 1872: S. 123—Privilege &-Action taken under Art. 356 of the Constitution of India-Government justifying its action-Whether could claim privilege under Administrative Law: Judicial Review-Whether confined to the decision making process only and not the decision itself merits-Justiciability and judicial review-Difference between.

Words & Phrases: 'Federalism' 'Federation' 'federal form of Government' 'Secularism' 'Judicial Review'-Meaning of in the context of the provisions of the Constitution of India.

In the present appeals and Transferred cases, the dissolution of the Legislative Assemblies in Karnataka, Rajasthan, Madhya Pradesh, Himachal Pradesh, Meghalaya and Nagaland, was challenged.

The expansion of Ministry in Karnataka (headed by Shri S.R. Bommai of Janata Dal) caused dissatisfaction to some of the aspirants. 20 MLAs later defected the part and write to the Governor on April 17, 1989 expressing no confidence in the leadership of Shri Bommai. The Governor sent a report to the President in April 19, 1989. Subsequently on April 20, · 1989, 7 out of the 20 MLAs wrote to the Governor that their signatures were obtained by misrepresentation and reaffirmed their support in Sb. Bommai. On the same day the Cabinet decided to convene the Assembly on April 27, 1989 to obtain vote of confidence and Shri Bommai met the Governor and requested him to allow floor test, so that he could prove his majority and that he was prepared even to advance the date of the session. The Governor sent his second report to the President, who exercising his power under Art. 356 issued proclamation dissolved the Assembly and assumed the administration of the State of Karnataka. A writ petition was filed challenging this and the High Court dismissed the writ petition, against which the present appeal is filed.

In the elections held in February, 1990, the Bhartiya Janta Party (BJP) emerged as the majority part in the legislative assemblies of Uttar Pradesh, Madhya Pradesh, Rajasthan and Himachal Pradesh, and formed governments in the said States. As per the manifesto of BJP, it was to construct a temple for Lord Sri Rama at his birth place Ayodhya. On December 6, 1992 the disputed Ram Janambhoomi Babri Masjid structure was demolished by the Karsewaks gathered at Ayodhya, as a result of sustained momentum generated by BJP, Vishva Hindu Parishad, Rashtriya Swayamsewak Sangh, Bajrang Dal, Shivsena and other organisations, despite the assurance given to this Court by the State Government that the disputed structure would be protected. Though the Government of U.P. resigned, the President issued a proclamation under Art. 356 of the Constitution and dissolved the U.P. State Assembly. Loss of precious lives of innocent people and property throughout the country and the neighbouring countries followed the demolition. The President exercising the power under Art. 356 issued proclamations, dismissed the State Governments of Rajasthan, Madhya Pradesh and Himachal Pradesh and dissolved the legislative assemblies or the States. These proclamations are also under challenge before this Court.

In the State of Meghalaya, the then Speaker of the House was elected as leader of the opposition group and he claimed the support of the majority of the members in the house and requested the governor to invite him to form the government. The Governor requested him to prove his majority on the floor of the house. 30 members voted for him and 27 voted against him. Before announcing the result, the Speaker intimated the house that he had received a complaint against five independent MLAs. in the ruling Coalition alleging disqualification under the Anti-defection Law and that he was suspending their right to vote. There was an uproar and the session had to be adjourned. The Speaker sent notices to the live independent MLAs, and later disqualified them, but not on the ground alleged in the show cause notice.

On Governor's advice, the Chief Minister summoned the session of the assembly. The Speaker refused to send the notices of the session to the live MLAs disqualified by him. He also made arrangements to ensure that they were not allowed to enter the assembly. Four of the five members obtained stay orders from this Court against the Speaker's order. Again, the Assembly was summoned to meet on October 8, 1991. The four MLAs. filed Contempt Petition against the Speaker; and on this Court's orders, they were invited to the session, and voted in favor of the motion expressing confidence in the Government. Excluding the votes of the said four members, the speaker declared that the Government had lost the confidence of the House. The Governor reported that a situation had arisen where the Government of the State cannot be carried on in accordance with the provisions of the Constitution and the President dismissed the Government on the basis of the report. This has been challenged before this Court.

In Nagaland, the Congress(I) party formed the Government in 1987, with 35 MLAs. In 1988, there was a split and 13 MLAs formed a separate party called Congress Ruling Party. It claimed the support of 35 MLAs and stated its claim to form the Ministry. The Governor sent a report to the President detailing the horse trading machinations and some MLAs having contact with the insurgents. The Chief Minister resigned and the Governor recommended imposition or President's Rule. President issued the proclamation under Art. 356 assuming the functions of the State of Nagaland. The dissident leader filed a writ petition challenging the proclamation. The Judges in the Division Bench differed on the scope of Art. 74(2) and S.123 of the Evidence Act and the matter was referred to a third Judge. However, before he could hear the matter, the Union of India filed Special Leave Petition and this Court granted leave and stayed the proceedings of the High Court.

Detailed arguments were advanced on the scope of Articles 356, especially in the context of related provisions viz. Arts. 354, 355, 357, 360, 154, 155, 159, 163 etc. and the approval of the proclamation by the Parliament. Arguments were also advanced on the scope and extent of Art. 74(2)as also S. 123 of the Evidence Act. Various contentions had been raised on Preamble to the Constitution, Federal structure of the Constitution, Judicial Review, Centre-State relations, basic structure of the Constitution as also secularism.

• • •

CHAPTER IX

L. CHANDRA KUMAR Vs. UNION OF INDIA AND OTHERS DECEMBER 2, 1994

Citations: [1994] 6 Suppl. SCR 261, (1995) 1 SCC 400

[KULDIP SINGH, B. L. HANSARIA ANDS. B. MAJMUDAR, JJ.]

Constitution of India-Articles 324-A and 324-B Administrative Tribunals Act 1985-Section 5(6) Constitutional validity of-Matters arising out of judgement of Constitution Bench in S. P. Sampath Kumar v. Union of India, and subsequent decisions referred to larger Bench.

In a matter involving an examination of Section 5(6) of the Administrative Tribunals Act 1985, this Court was confronted with wider issues relating to the composition, jurisdiction, power and authority of Tribunals constituted under Articles 324-A and 324-B. Referring the matter to a larger Bench, this Court.

HELD: In view of the decision in S. P. Sampath Kumar's case, by which a Constitution Bench of this Court decided the vires of the Administrative Tribunals Act 1985, and observations made therein, the ·matter be placed before a larger Bench for reconsideration. Subsequent decisions on matters adjudicated upon in Sampath Kumar are also referred to the larger Bench.

The issues referred to larger Bench include.

1. Whether Tribunals can be equated with High Courts. (263 BJ

2. The jurisdiction, power and authority of Administrative Tribunals to adjudicate upon questions of constitutional validity of legislations and of rules. [263 CJ

3. Whether a Tribunal which has the power to decide on the constitutional validity of a statute or rule made under Article 309 can have an Administrative Member on its Bench. [265 CJ

4. Whether the power of judicial review held to be available to Administrative Tribunals as per Sampath Kumar's Case violates the basic structure of the Constitution. [263 HJ

• • •

CHAPTER X

VELLORE CITIZENS WELFARE FORUM Vs. UNION OF INDIA AND ORS. AUGUST 28, 1996

Citations: [1996] 5 Suppl. SCR 241, (1996) 5 SCC 647

[KULDIP SINGH, FAIZAN UDDIN AND K. VENKATASWAMI, JJ.)

Environmental Law

Constitution of India, 1950: Articles 21, 47, 48-A and 51-A(g). Environmental pollution-Caused by tanneries-Untreated effluent by tanneries in State of Tamil Nadu---Discharge of-Thereby polluted sub-soil liver water resulting in non-availability of potable water-Spoiled physico-chemical properties of soil, making it unfit for cultivation-Held : even though such industries were of vital importance to country, they could not be permitted to continue their production unless pollution control devices were set up by, them-Having regard to pollution caused by them, principle of Sustainable Development had to be accepted as a balancing concept--Precautionary Principle and Polluter Pays Principle acceptable as part of environmental law of country and should be implemented--Precautionary environmental measures should be taken by State Government and statutory authorities and lack of scientific certainty could not be ground for postponing such measures to prevent environmental degradation-Onus of proof' was on polluting E industries to show that their actions were environmentally benign-Such polluting industries liable to pay compensation for past pollution generated by them-Pollution fine of Rs. 10,000 imposed on each tannery-Money to be deposited in "Environment Protection Fund" to be utilised for compensating affected persons and rest01ing damaged environment.

A1ticles 32 and 226-Public Interest Litigation-Environmental Pollution-Caused by tanneries in State of Tamil Nadu-Comprehensive directions issued by Supreme Court---However, instead of Supreme Court itself monitoring the matter any further, Madras High Court advised to constitute a "Green Bench" to deal with all environmental matters in future-Such "Green Benches" already functioning in some High Courts.

Environment (Protection) Act, 1986: Section 3(3)-Authority-Central Government directed to constitute Authority to be headed by a retired High Court Judge-Authority to have all powers necessary to deal with situation created by tanneries and polluting industries in State of Tamil Nadu- Authority to compute compensation payable by polluting industries to affected individuals and that payable for restoring damaged environment- Authority also to frame scheme in consultation with expert bodies like NEERJ, Central Board and State Board for reversing damage caused to ecology and environment.

International Law: Customary International Law-Rules of -Held: if not contrary to Municipal Law, deemed to be incorporated in domestic Law.

The petitioner filed a Public Interest Petition under Article 32 of the Constitution against the pollution which was being caused by enormous discharge of untreated effluent by the tanneries and other industries in the State of Tamil Nadu. The tanneries were discharging untreated effluent into agricultural fields, road-sides, waterways and open lands. The untreated effluent was finally discharged in the river which was the main source of water supply to the residents of the areas. The entire surface and sub-soil water of the river had been polluted resulting in non-availability of potable water to the residents of the, area. The tanneries in the State of Tamil Nadu had caused environmental degradation in the area. According to the preliminary survey made by the Tamil Nadu Agricultural University Research Centre nearly 35, 000 hectares of agricultural land in the Tanneries Belt, had become either partially or totally unfit for cultivation. The tanneries used about 170 types of chemicals in the chrome tanning processes. Nearly 35 liters of water was used for processing one kilogram of finished leather, resulting in dangerously enormous quantities of toxic effluents being let out in the open by the tanning industry. These effluents had spoiled the physio-chemical properties of the soil, and had contaminated ground water by percolation. An independent survey conducted by Peace Members, a non-governmental organisation, covering 13 villages of the State revealed that 350 wells out of a total of 467 used for drinking and irrigation purposes had been polluted. Women and children have to walk miles to get drinking water.

The tanneries and other polluting industries in the State of Tamil Nadu were being persuaded for the last 10 years by the State Government and the Tamil Nadu Pollution Control Board to control the pollution generated by them. They were given option either to construct common effluent treatment plants for a cluster of industries or to set up individual pollution control devices. The Central Government agreed to give substantially subsidy for the construction of common effluent treatment plants (CETPs).

However, till date most of the tanneries operating in the State of Tamil Nadu had not taken any step to control the pollution caused by the discharge of effluent.

• • •

CHAPTER XI

D.K. BASU Vs. STATE OF WEST BENGAL DECEMBER 18, 1996

Citations: [1996] 10 Suppl. SCR 284, (1997) 1 SCC 416

[KULDIP SINGH AND DR. A.S. ANAND, JJ.]

Constitution of India, 1950: Articles 21, 22 and 32.

Custodial violence-Torture, rape and death in police custody/lockup-Infringes Art. 21 as well as basic human rights and strikes a blow at rule of law-Torture involved not only physical suffering but also mental agony-It was naked violation of human dignity and destruction of human personality-interrogation must be sustained and scientific-Third-degree methods would be impermissible--Balanced approach needed to meet ends of justice so that criminals did not go scot-free-Custodial deaths was one of the worst crimes in civilised society Transparency of action and accountability were two safe-guards to check abuse of police power-State terrorism was no answer to terrorism-Victim of custodial violence and in case of his death in custody, his f amity members entitled to compensation under public law in addition to remedy available under private law for damages for tortious act of police personnel-Mandatory 'requirements' issued by Supreme Court shall be complied with by police personnel while arresting or detaining any person-These were in addition to constitutional and statutory directions-The requirements would apply with equal force to all governmental agencies-The requirements must be circulated to all police stations and publicised through mass media-Failure to comply with the requirements would render the official concerned liable for departmental action as well as contempt of court-Proceedings for contempt of court could be instituted in High Court having territorial jurisdiction-Penal Code, 1860, Ss. 220, 330 and · 331.

Fundamental Rights-Established invasion of-Compensation for-Held: Compensation could be awarded under public law by Supreme ' Court and by High Courts in addition to traditional remedies under private law for tortious acts and punishment to wrongdoer under criminal law.

Public law proceedings-Object of-Held: Different from private law proceedings-Award of compensation in public law proceedings, in a given case, could be adjusted against damages awarded in a civil suit.

The petitioner filed a petition-public interest-in this Court in the wake of news items published in the Telegraph, the Statesman and the Indian Express regarding deaths in police lock-up and custody. The petition stated that efforts were often made to hush up the lock-up deaths and thus the crime went unpunished and "flourished". On behalf of the petitioner it was submitted that modalities for awarding compensation to the victim and/or family members of the victim for atrocities and death caused in police custody and to provide for accountability of the officers concerned be formulated.

• • •

CHAPTER XII

MAFATLAL INDUSTRIES LTD. ETC. ETC. Vs. UNION OF INDIA ETC. DECEMBER 19, 1996

Citations: [1996] 10 Suppl. SCR 585, (1997) 5 SCC 536

(A. M. AHMADI, 0., J.S. VERMA, S.C. AGRAWAL, B.P. JEEVAN REDDY, DR. A.S. ANAND, B.L. HANSARIA, S.C. SEN, K.S. PARIPOORNAN AND B.N. KIRPAL, JJ.]

Excise/Customs: Excise/Customs duty levied on misrepresentation/ misapplication/erroneous interpretation of the statutory provisions under provisions declared unconstitutional or under mistake of law-Remedies open--Maintainability of suit under S. 72 of Contract Act or writ petition under Art. 226 or Art. 32 or other remedies provided in Excise Act or Customs Act-Held, where refund is claimed on the ground that provisions of the Central Excises Act/Customs Act whereunder duty levied is or held to be unconstitutional, suit or writ petition would be maintainable-However, all refund claims must be filed and adjudicated under the Central Excises Act or the Customs Act-In such cases suit invoking S. 72 of Contract Act would be barred-Writ jurisdiction in such cases to be exercised in accordance with the legislative intent manifested in the Act-in all situations refund can only be allowed where manufacturer assesses has not passed on the burden of tax to third parties viz. consumers-Presumption is of passing on the burden to the consumers-Burden on the manufacturer to rebut the presumption by establishing to the contrary-Doctrine of undue enrichment applicable to such assesses but not F applicable to State-Contract Act, 1872, S.72.

Excise duty paid under a provision declared unconstitutional----Petitioner failing to assail its constitutionality and the decision becoming final-Declaration of unconstitutionality obtained by another person on another ground-Held cannot be availed of by such petitioner to reopen the decision in his case.

Excise duty paid under a provision declared unconstitutional----Petitioner failing to assail its constitutionality and the decision becoming final-Declaration of unconstitutionality obtained by another person on another ground-Held cannot be availed of by such petitioner to reopen the decision in his case. Excise duty paid under mistake of law-Refund-

Maintainability of suit or writ petition-Held, Once assessment or levy became final in case of a manufacturer- assesses, he cannot later file suit or writ petition claiming refund on the ground that decision of Court or Tribunal in another person's case led him to discover the mistake of law under which he paid the duty. In all cases where suit or writ petition is open, it is necessary for the plaintiff / petitioner to file suit or writ petition within the limitation period under S.17(1)(c) of Limitation Act and to allege and establish that he has not B passed on the burden of tax to the consumer-Where claim has to be made under the Central Excises Act or Customs Act, and no suit lies, such claim to be preferred within the period of limitation prescribed under the said Acts—Limitation Act, 1963, S.17(1)(c).

State can raise plea in defense, of spending away the amount of tax collected under unconstitutional law and/or of financial chaos in administration of the State, as a result of allowing claim of refund-Such plea by assesses not tenable where he has not passed on the burden of duty to others.

State cannot reclaim the refunded amounts where no proceedings are pending-All pending matters to be governed by the law declared in the present case notwithstanding any refunds made in such pending proceedings.

Excise Law: Central Excises and Salt Act, 1944-Ss.11-B, 11-C, 12-A, 12-B, 12-C, E 12-D Validity of-Held, valid-S.11-B not a device to retain illegally collected duty Ss.11-B and 12-B have the effect of changing the very nature of excise duty.

S.11-B-Retrospective operation-Refund-Tax levied under mistake of F law-Limitation-Held, S.11-B applies to all pending proceedings but not to those proceedings which have become final after appeal period expired before the commencement of the 1991 Amendment Act-Application for refund under S.11-B to be made within six months from date of payment of duty -Since this requirement cannot be complied with in respect of pending 'G decrees or orders, to ensure that such orders and decrees are not frustrated, it must be deemed that the duties were paid 'under protest' within the meaning of second proviso to S.11- B(l)-Customs Act. 1962, S.27.

Central Excise Rules, 1944-R.233-B- Grounds for payment of duty under protest ---Assesses need not particularise the grounds ---- letter of protest acknowledged by the officer shall be [proof of payment duty under protests under S.11-B of the Central Excises and Salt Act.

Constitution of India, 1950: Art. 14-Taxing Statutes-Discretion of the Legislature-State allowed to pick and choose districts, objects, persons, methods and even rates for taxation with reasonableness-Courts view laws relating to economic activities with greater latitude than other matters.

Arts, 14 and 19--Reasonableness of a statutory provision-Mere possibility of abuse by those in charge of administering it-Not a ground for holding it procedurally or substantively unreasonable-Administrative Law-Judicial Review.

Art. 226-rHigh Court to exercise its writ jurisdiction in consonance with the legislative intent manifested by the statutory provisions involved-Jurisdiction under Art. 226 to be exercised to effectuate the regime of law and not to abrogate it.-Maintainability of writ petitio1t-Altemative remedy-Refund claim against tax/duty wrongly paid-Remedy under the relevant Act alone to be pursued-Central Excises and Salt Act, 1944, S.11: B-Customs Act, 1962, S.27.

Article 265-Tax levied or collected contrary to law-Refund of-Where taxing statute provides for refund, validity of such provision must be examined with reference to other provisions of the Constitution-Where refund is claimed on the ground that tax has been paid under mistake of law, claimant assesses must plead and prove that he has not passed on the tax burden to third persons. _Contract Act, 1872:

S. 72-Action for restitution under-Based on equity-Person claiming restitution must plead and prove that he suffered loss or injury-Burden of proof on petitioner/plaintiff since the fact whether duty passed on or not is within his special and exclusive knowledge-If assesses passes on the tax burden to third persons, no suit for refund on ground of mistake of law would be maintainable Evidence Act, 1872 : S.106-Sale of Goods Act. 1930.

S.64-A.

Civil Procedure Code, 190 &-S.9-Civil Court's Jurisdiction-Bar of by implication-Suit not maintainable where a complete mechanism for redressal is provided by the statute concerned-Central Excises and Salt Act, 1944, S.11-B-Customs Act, 1962, S.27.

DOCTRINES-Doctrine of unjust enrichment-Doctrine of restitution-Discussed.

WORDS AND PHRASES-..."Tax"--"Levy"-"Jurisdiction"--"jurisdictional error"-Meaning of.

The present appeals and writ petitions raised certain questions concerning the refund of Excise & Customs duty collected contrary to law.

These questions related to the correctness of certain earlier decisions of Supreme Court, concept of unjust enrichment, interpretation of Article 265 of the Constitution of India and of the provisions of the Central Excises and Salt Act 1944 and the Customs Act 1962.

The main topic of controversy viz. refund of Excise duty was governed by different provisions over the years; viz.(i) upto August 6, 1977, the refund of duties was governed by Rule 11, as it stood upto that date;(ii) between August 6, 1977 and November 16, 1980 refund of duties was governed by Rule 11 as it obtained during the said period; (iii) from November 16, 1980 upto September 19, 1991 (date of coming into force of 1991 Amendment Act) the refund of duties was governed by Section 11B as it stood during the said period; (iv) with effect from September 19, 1991 the refund of duties is governed by Section 11B as amended by the 1991 Amendment Act and the allied provisions. Though different provisions governed the subject of refund during different times, there is one feature uniformly common to all of them viz. they purport to be exhaustive on subject of refund and they provided a period of limitation for making such claims.

In these appeals and writ petitions the appellants/writ petitioners contended that the provisions relating to refund of excise/customs duty did not preclude the filing of a suit or the filing of a writ petition claiming refund where tax has been collected contrary to law by virtue of Article 265 of the Constitution and that the question of passing on the burden of duty is totally irrelevant in the matter of refund; that the law laid down in Kanhaiya Lal has been the law over the last 37 years and has been followed consistently by different Benches of the Supreme Court and that there were no good or compelling reasons to deviate from or to overrule the decision in Kanhaiya Lal; referring. to the second alternative condition imposed by Section 424 wherein it was provided that if the manufacturer gives a bond undertaking to refund the same to purchaser within a particular period he would be entitled to claim the refund, it was urged that such a condition could have been imposed in the Central Excises and Customs Act as well; that even if it is legitimate for Parliament to prescribe that in case the money was Passed on it must be made over to the person from whom it was collected, and this should be done through the medium of manufacturer/ tax payer and not through any other medium; that a claim for refund has to be filed within six months from the relevant date but since appellate/ revision proceedings or for that matter proceedings in High Court/Supreme

Court take number of years and by the time the claimant succeeds and asks for refund his claim will be barred and it will be thrown out on the ground that it has not been filed within six months from the date of payment of duty; that Rule 233B which prescribes the procedure to be followed in cases where duty is paid under protest requires the assesses to state the grounds for payment of duty under protest and that it may well happen that the authority to. whom the letter of protest is submitted may refuse to record it if he is not satisfied with the grounds of protest; that the amended Section 11B is prospective in operation and cannot apply to pending proceedings; that Section 12A was also inserted by the 1991 (Amendment) Act and therefore it is not expected of any manufacturer/assesses to maintain the records required by Section 12A prior to its coming into force; that in respect of an application filed before the commencement of the said Act it is not possible to comply with the requirements of sub-section (1) in so far as it requires the filing of documents referred to in Section 12A and this circumstance was urged as a ground for holding that the amended Section llB applies only to refund applications filed after coming into force of the 1991 (Amendment) Act; that tile right to recover the excise duty paid is both a constitutional and a statutory right; and that all these factors militate against giving retrospective effect to Section 11B.

It was also submitted that the real purpose behind Section 11B and its allied provisions was not to benefit the consumers by refusing refund to manufacturer (on the ground of passing on the burden) but only to enable the Government to retain the illegally collected taxes; that the creation of the Consumer Welfare Fund is a mere pretense and not an honest exercise; that as per Section 12D even a Consumer who has really borne the burden of tax and is in a position to establish that fact is yet not entitled to apply for refund of the duty since the Rules do not provide for such a situation; that there is no provision in the Act to locate the person really entitled to refund and to make over the money to him; that in a competitive atmosphere and for other commercial reasons it may happen that the manufacture is obliged to sell his goods at less than its proper price and the manufacturer may have to forego not only his profit but also part of excise duty and that in such a case levy and collection of full excise duty would cease to be a duty of excise and it will become a tax on income or on business; that Section 11D provides for double taxation and that sub-section (i) of Section 11D makes the manufacturer liable to pay duty which he collects from the buyer as part of the price of goods even where the manufacturer has already paid the duty at the time of removal of the goods.

On behalf of the Union of India it was contended that Kanhaiya Lal has been wrongly decided; that no suit or writ petition lies for refund of duty except in the case of unconstitutional levy and even in such cases the claim is subject to proof that burden of duty has not been passed on to the purchaser; that in all other cases claims of refund can be· made only under and in accordance with the provisions of the Act/Rules governing the subject of refund and in no other manner and in no other forum; that in any event since Kanhaiya Lal did not deal with the effect of passing on the duty to a third party it was neither raised nor considered therein; hence it is no authority for the proposition that the manufacturer/payer can recover the duty paid even if he has passed on the burden to others; that the distinction between the constitutional values obtaining in countries like United States of America, Canada and Australia or United Kingdom and the values obtaining under our Constitution are different; that the philosophy and the core values of our Constitution must be kept in mind while understanding and applying the provisions of Art. 265 of the Constitution and Section 72 of the Contract Act that it ill becomes the manufacturers/assesses to espouse the cause of consumers when all the while they had been making a killing at their expense; that no consumer organisation had come forward to voice any grievance against the relevant provisions; that clause (e) of the proviso to sub-section (2) of Section 118 did provide for the buyer of the goods to whom the burden of duty has been passed on to apply for refund of duty to him, provided that he has not in his turn passed on the duty to others and therefore it was not correct to suggest that the Act did not provide for refund of duty to the person who has actually borne the burden; that there in novice in the relevant provisions of the Act; that Rules cannot be relied upon to impugn the validity of an enactment, which must stand or fall on its own strength; that the defect in the Rules if any, could always be corrected if the experience warrant it; that the Court may indicate the modification needed in the Rules and that the Government is always prepared to make appropriate changes in the Rules since it views the process as a trial and error method; and that in case a manufacturer is obliged to sell his goods at a price lower than the normal price declared under S.4 it is always open to him to approach the excise authorities for redetermination of the assessable value.

• • •

CHAPTER XIII

VISHAKA AND ORS. Vs. STATE OF RAJASTHAN AND ORS. AUGUST 13, 1997

Citations: [1997] 3 Suppl. SCR 404, (1997) 6 SCC 241

[J.S. VERMA C J, SUJATA V. MANOHARAND B.N. KIRPAL, JJ.]

Constitution of India-Articles 14, 15, 19 and 21-Fundamental Rights-Working Women-Gender Equality-Sexual harassment of working women in work places-Held, such incidents result in violation of 'gender equality' as also Right to life and liberty and the right to practice profession or to carry out occupation, trade or business. Articles 51 (c), 253--Power of Parliament to enact laws-Absence of domestic law occupying the field-Value and significance of the International Convention and norms-Held, the International Convention and norms are of great significance and Parliament has the power to enact laws for implementing the same.

Articles 32, 141-Power of the Supreme Court to enforce Fundamental Rights-To lay down guidelines and norms in the absence of any legislation-Held, Supreme Court has power to lay down guidelines and norms for due observance in work places or institutions, until a legislation is enacted and such norms would be treated as law. The present petition was filed for the enforcement of fundamental Rights of working women under Articles 14, 19 and 21 of the Constitution of India. It was brought as a class action by certain social activists and NGOs with the aim of focusing attention towards societal. aberration and assisting in finding suitable methods for realisation of the true concept of 'gender equality'; to prevent sexual harassment of working women in all work places through judicial process, and to fill the vacuum in existing legislation. The immediate cause for the filing of present petition was an incident of alleged brutal gang rape of a social worker in a village in Rajasthan.

• • •

CHAPTER XIV

GITHA HARIHARAN AND ANR Vs. RESERVE BANK OF INDIA AND ANR. FEBRUARY 17, 1999

Citations: [1999] 1 SCR 669, (1999) 2 SCC 228

[DR. A.S. ANAND, C.J., M. SRINIVASAN AND BUMESH C. BANERJEE, JJ.)

Hindu Law: Hindu Minority and Guardianship Act, 1956 Section 6(a)-Provided that mother had the right to become a natural guardian of a minor only 'after' the father-Discrimination on ground of sex alone-Constitutionality of-Mother and father of a minor jointly applied to the Reserve Bank of India (RBI) for opening a deposit account in the name of the minor-Mother, in agreement with the father, signed the application as the guardian of the minor-But RBI refused to accept the application on the ground that the mother, during the lifetime of the f other, was not the natural guardian of the mother-Held, legislature is presumed to act in accordance with the Constitution-Hence, Section 6(a) can be constituted in such a manner so as to retain it within constitutional limits-Moreover, if Ss. 4 and 6 of the HMG Act are construed anomalously, the word 'after' means 'in the absence of thereby refencing to the father's absence from the care of the minor's property or person for any reason whatever-Hence, in such situations the mother can validity act as the natural guardian of the minor even during the lifetime of the father who is considered to be absent-Therefore, RBI was not right in refusing to accept the said application-However, this judgment is to operate prospectively -All organisations are directed to formulate appropriate methodology accordingly-Same decision to apply in respect of guardianship under S. 19(b) of the GW Act-Constitution of India, 1950, Alts, 14 and 15--Guardians and Wards Act, 1890, S 19(b)-Convention on the Elimination of All Forms of Discrimination Against Women, 1979 ("CEDAW')--Beijing Declaration.

Section 2-Scope and ambit of-Held, the law relating to minority and guardianship amongst Hindus is to be found not only in the old Hindu law as laid down by the smritis, shrutis and the commentaries as recognised by the Courts of law but also statutes applicable amongst others to Hindus viz., Guardian and Wards Act, 1890 and Indian Majority Act, 1875 Jurisprudence of-importance of-Held, Hindu law has shown no signs of decrepitude and it has its values and importance even today-However; certain parts of Hindu law is codified to give fitful meaning and statutory sanction to the prevailing concept of law having due regard to the social and economic charges in the society.

Constitution of India, 1950: Article 51-Scope of-Held, when there is no inconsistency between domestic and international laws, courts are obliged to give due regard to international conventions and norms while costuming domestic laws.

Interpretation of Statutes: Basic rules --Held, where two interpretations are possible the Court should lean infavour of the statutory provision. General mines-Held, narrow pedantic interpretation naming counter to the constitutional mandate ought to be avoided always-If such interpretation departs from the legislative enactment, a wider debate is called for having due regard to contextual facts.

Subsidiary rules-Presumptions-Held, validity of a legislation is to be presumed-Only in the event of gross violation of constitutional sanctions that the law courts would be within its jurisdiction to declare the legislative enactment to be an invalid piece of legislation and not otherwise.

Internal aids-Definition Clause-Scope of-Held, same meaning ought to be attributed to the same word used by the statute as per the definition Section.

Words and Phrases: ''After"--Meaning of-In the context of S.6(a) of the Hindu Minority and Guardianship Act, 1956.

"Guardian''-Meaning of-In the context of S.4(b) of the Hindu Minority and Guardianship Act, 1956.

"Natural Guardian "---Meaning of-In the context of S.4(c) of the Hindu Minority and Guardianship Act, 1956.

The first petitioner and her husband, the second petitioner, jointly applied to the Reserve Bank of India, the first respondent, for issue of Relief Bonds in the name of their minor son. The petitioners stated expressly that both of them agreed that the mother of the child, i.e., the first petitioner would act as the guardian of the minor for the purpose of investments made with the money held by their minor son. Accordingly, in the prescribed form of application, the first petitioner signed as the guardian of the minor. The first respondent replied to the petitioners advising them either to produce the application form signed by the father of the minor or a certificate of guardianship from a competent authority in favour of the mother and refused to accept the deposit from the petitioners.

Being aggrieved the petitioners filed a writ petition No. 489/95 before this Court with prayers to strike down Section 6(a) of the Hindu Minority and Guardianship Act, 1956 (HMG Act) and Section 19(b) of the Guardian and Wards Act, 1890 (GW Act) as violative of Articles 14 and 15 of the Constitution and to quash and set aside the decision of the first respondent refusing to accept the deposit from the petitioners and to issue a mandamus directing the acceptance of the of the same after declaring the first petitioner as the natural guardian of the minor.

In writ petition No. 1018/91 filed before this Court, the petitioner is the wife of the first respondent. The first respondent instituted a proceeding for divorce against the petitioner and it was pending in the District Court. The first respondent had also prayed for custody of their minor son in the same proceeding. The petitioner had in turn filed an application for maintenance for herself and the minor son. The first respondent had been repeatedly writing to the petitioner and the school in which the minor was studying, asserting that the first respondent was the only natural guardian of the minor and no decision should be taken without his permission. The minor son was staying with the petitioner and, in spite of the best efforts of the petitioner, the father had shown total apathy towards the child and as a matter of fact was not interested in the welfare and benefit of the child excepting, however, claiming the right to be the natural guardian without, however, discharging any corresponding obligation. The petitioner, therefore, filed the present writ petition before this Court challenging the constitutionality of Section 6(a) of the HMG Act and Section 19(b) of the GW Act.

On behalf of the petitioner it was contended that the two Sections i.e. Section 6(a) of HMG Act and Section 19(b) of GW Act were violative of the equality clause of the Constitution, inasmuch as the mother of the minor is .relegated to an inferior position on the ground of sex alone since her right, as a natural guardian of the minor, was made cognisable only 'after' the father, and, therefore, both the Sections must be struck down as unconstitutional.

On behalf of the respondents it was contended that the mother was not the natural guardian of the minor son and that it was also stated under Section 6(a) of the HMG Act that the father of a Hindu Minor was the only natural guardian of the minor.

• • •

CHAPTER XV

RUPA ASHOK HURRA Vs. ASHOK HURRA AND ANR. APRIL 10, 2002

Citations: [2002] 2 SCR 1006, (2002) 4 SCC 388

[S.P. BHARUCHA, CJ., SYED SHAH MOHAMMED QUADRI, UMESH C. BANERJEE, S.N. VARIA VA AND SHIVARAJ V. PATIL, JJ.]

Constitution of India, 1950: Articles 12 and 32-Writ Petition-Writ of certiorari-Challenging validity of judgment of Supreme Court after dismissal of Review Petition there in-Maintainability of-Held, not maintainable-Superior Courts of Justice do not fall under the ambit of State or other authorities under Article 12.

Article 142-Reconsideration of Judgment of Supreme Court after dismissal of Review Petition-Permissibility under inherent powers-Held, Court may reconsider its judgments in exercise of its inherent powers in rarest of rare cases to prevent abuse of its process and to cure gross miscarriage of justice-Grounds and procedure for such re-consideration laid down-Supreme Court Rules, 1966-0rder XL VII Rule 6.

Doctrines: Doctrine of Ex debito Justitiae-Applicability of Doctrine of stare decisis-discussed. The common questions for consideration in the instant writ petitions were whether writ petition under Article 32 of the Constitution of India could be maintained to question the validity of a Judgment of Supreme Court after the petition for review of the said judgment was dismissed; and whether the order passed by this Court could be corrected under its inherent powers after dismissal of the review petition on the ground that it was passed either without jurisdiction or in violation of the principles of natural justice or due to unfair procedure giving scope for bias which resulted in abuse of the process of the Court or miscarriage of justice to an aggrieved person.

• • •

CHAPTER XVI

PRADEEP KUMAR BISWAS AND ORS. Vs. INDIAN INSTITUTE OF CHEMICAL BIOLOGY AND ORS. APRIL 16, 2002

Citations: [2002] 3 SCR 100, (2002) 5 SCC 111

[S.P. BHARUCHA, CJ., SYED SHAH MOHAMMED QUADRI, R.C. LAHOTI; N. SANTOSH HEGDE, DORAISWAMY RAJU, RUMA PAL AND ARIJIT PASAYAT, JJ.]

Constitution of India, I950-Article I2-Council of Scientific and Industrial Research (CSIR)-Whether a 'State '-Held, it is 'State' falling within the range of the Article as per the tests judicially evolved for the purpose Notification bringing CSIR within purview of Section 14(2) of Administrative Tribunals Act, I985 is conclusive of the fact that CSIR is a state within the meaning of Article I 2.

Precedent-Normally a precedent which has stood for a length of time should not be reversed however erroneous the reasoning is, if it has stood unquestioned-But in the facts of the case, Sabhajit Tewary' case cannot stand as an authority since the decision was plainly erroneous-It is Court's duty not to perpetuate its mistake.

Appellants-employees of a Unit of Council of Scientific and Industrial Research (CSIR) had filed Writ Petition challenging their termination from service. High Court dismissed the same in view of Sabhajit Tewary 's case wherein it was held that writ petition against CSIR was not maintainable as it was not an authority within the meaning of Article 12 of the Constitution of India.

In appeal to this Court, the matter was referred to the Constitution Bench for reconsideration of Sabhajit Tewary's case having regard to the pronouncement of this Court in several subsequent decisions in respect of several other institutes of similar nature set up by Union of India.

Thus the question for consideration was whether CSIR is a State within the meaning of Article 12 of the Constitution.

• • •

CHAPTER XVII

P. RAMA CHANDRA RAO Vs. STATE OF KARNATAKA APRIL 16, 2002

Citations: [2002] 3 SCR 60, (2002) 4 SCC 578

(S.P. BHARUCHA, CJ. SYED SHAH MOHAMMED QUADRI, R.C. LAHOTI, N. SANTOSH HEGDE, DORAISWAMY RAJU, RUMA PAL AND ARIJIT PASAYAT, JJ.]

Constitution of India, 1950-Article 21-Right to speedy trial-Criminal Proceedings-Limitation bar provided by judgment of smaller Benches of Supreme Court-Held, such bar contrary to law laid down by larger Bench in Antulay's case-Limitation bars not good law, since the same would amount to impermissible legislation and contrary to law of precedent-To effectuate the right to speedy trial, powers under Sections 309, 311, 258 and 482 of Code of Criminal Procedure and Articles 226 and 227 of Constitution could be exercised-Code of Criminal Procedure, 1973-Sections 309, 311, 258 and 482.

Doctrines: Doctrine of precedent-Pronouncements by smaller Benches contrary to law laid down by larger Bench-Smaller Bench is bound by view expressed by larger Bench.

Judicial Review:

Held, is restricted to declaring and interpreting law and removing obvious

1.wicunae and filling the gaps-Not to entrench upon the field of legislation which is meant for legislature-Constitution of India, ...J950-Articles 32, 21, 141, 142-Code of Criminal Procedure, 1973-Chapter XXXVI.

In Common Cause v. Union of India, [1996) 4 SCC 33, (Common Cause I); Common Cause v. Union of India, [1996) 6 SCC 775 (Common Cause II); Rajdev Sharma v. State of Bihar, [1998) 7 SCC (Raj Dev Sharma I); Raj Dev Sharma II v. State of Bihar, [1999) 7 SCC 604 (Raj Dev Sharma II), the Court had issued direction fixing outer time limits for conclusion of certain nature of criminal proceedings.

In the instant appeals, accused facing corruption charges were acquitted by special courts in terms of directions in Raj Dev Sharma I case as there was failure of commencement of trial despite lapse of two years from the date of framing of the charges. The appeals of the State against the acquittal were allowed by High Court without issuing notice to the respective accused.

In appeal to this Court, the question for consideration arose as to whether earlier decisions of this Court, in Common Cause I. Common Cause lI, Raj Dev Sharma I Raj Dev Sharma II cases would apply to prosecution under Prevention of Corruption Act, 1988 and other economic offences. The case was, therefore, referred to a Constitution Bench.

During the hearing, the Constitution Bench was of the opinion that the directions in the Common Cause cases and Raj Dev Sharma cases ran counter to Constitution Bench directions in A.R. Antulay 's case, which had laid down the law that an outer time limit for conclusion of all criminal proceedings should not be drawn or prescribed. Since A.R Antulay's case was decided by Bench of 5 Judges the instant case was referred to seven Judges Bench.

The question for consideration therein was whether a Court in its zeal to protect the right to speedy trial of an accused, can devise and almost enact such bars of limitation though the legislature and the statutes have not chosen to do so.

• • •

CHAPTER XVIII

T. M. A. PAI FOUNDATION AND ORS. Vs. STATE OF KARNATAKA AND ORS. OCTOBER 31, 2002

Citations: [2002] 3 Suppl. SCR 587, (2002) 8 SCC 481, AIR 2003 SC 355

[B.N. KIRPAL, CJ., G.B PATTANAIK, V.N. KHARE, S. RAJENDRA BABU, SYED SHAH MOHAMMED QUADRI, RUMA PAL, S.N. V ARIA VA, K.G. BALAKRISHNAN, P. VENKATARAMA REDDI, ASHOK BHAN AND ARIJIT PASA YAT, JJ.]

Constitution of India, 1950: Article 30-Private Institutions-Government Regulations Applicability of and its extent-Held: in case of private unaided educational institution Government can put conditions pertaining to academic and educational matters and welfare of students and teachers only, but not in the matter of administration-In case of private aided educational institutions, once aid is granted, Government as a condition of grant of aid, can put letters on the freedom in the matter of administration and management of the institution-But such institutions cannot be treated as wholly owned and controlled by Government-Hence Government cannot interfere. with constitution of governing bodies-Autonomy of aided institution would be less than that of an unaided institution. Articles 29(2) and 30(1)-Right of Aided Private Minority Institution to Administer itself-Government regulation-Extent of applicability to Held, right under Article 30(1) is not absolute although right to administer includes right to grant admission to students of its choice-But when such minority institution is granted aid, Article 29(2) would apply-Hence one of the rights of administration of the minorities i.e. right to grant admission would be eroded to some extent-However, there is an interplay between the two Articles-Such an institution should admit non-minority students based on merit to a reasonable extent, whereby minority character of the institution is not annihilated and at the same time rights granted under Article 29(2)are not subverted-The reasonable extent would depend on variable factors and specific percentage cannot be fixed-Articles 28(1) and (3).

Article 30(2)-Meaning, Scope and effect of-Whether the provision gives a right to ask for grant and aid from the State-In case of State aided institution extent of its autonomy -Held, grant of aid is not a constitutional imperative-The provision means that grant of aid by State could not be denied to religious/linguistic minority institution only on the ground that the management of the institution is by minority-But if an abject surrender of right to management is. made a condition of aid, the denial of aid would be violative of the provision-However, conditions of aid that do not involve a surrender of substantial right of management would not be inconsistent with constitutional guarantees ev.en if they indirectly impinge upon some facts of administration-Article 337.

Article 30(1), VII Schedule List III Entry 2 5-Linguistic and Religious Minority-Unit of-Whether within the State or the country as a whole Held, it would be decided state-wise-Inclusion of 'education' in VII Schedule, List III Entry 25 would not affect determination of a "religious" or "linguistic" minority.

Articles 19(1)(g), 26 and 30-Establishment and administering of educational institution-Held: ls covered by these Articles and hence a fundamental right.

Articles 26 and 30-Difference between-Discussed.

Unnikrishnan 's case-Reconsideration of-Held, the case, in so far as it framed the scheme relating to grant of admission and fixing of fee, overruled.

Interpretation of Constitution-Harmonious construction-Held, when constitutional provisions are interpreted it has to be borne in mind that the interpretation should be such as to further the object for which they were incorporated-They cannot be read in isolation and have to be read harmoniously to provide meaning and purpose-They cannot be interpreted as to render another provision redundant-Purposive and harmonious interpretation required.

Interpretation of Statute-Historical facts and Constituent Assembly debates Aid of-Held, aid can be taken for construing the provisions of an Act or the Constitution.

Doctrines: Doctrine of real de facto equality-Applicability of

Words and Phrases: "Occupation"-Meaning of in the context of Article 19(/)(g) of the Constitution of India, I 950.

"Minority"-Meaning of "Religious and Linguistic Minority"-Meaning of in the context of Article 30 of the Constitution.

"Private educational institution "-Meaning of. Earlier, a 5 Judges Bench of this Court was of the view that Article 30 of the Constitution of India did not clothe a minority educational institution with power to adopt its own method of selection and doubted the correctness of the decision in St.

Stephen's College v. University of Delhi, [1992] 1 SCC 558. The matter was then placed before 7 Judges Bench who directed the matter to be placed before II Judges Bench because it felt that in view of 42nd Amendment to the Constitution, whereby "education" had been included in Entry 25 of List III of VII Schedule of the Constitution, the question as to who would be regarded as "minority" was required to be considered because the earlier cases deciding the issue related to pre-amendment era, when 'education' was only in State List.

Eleven questions were referred to the Constitution Bench. In view of the arguments led by the parties in the petitions, the following five main issues arose for consideration:

I. Is there a fundamental right to set up educational institutions and if so, under which provision?

2. Does Unnikrishnan 's case require reconsideration?

3. In case of private institutions, can there be Government Regulations and, if so, to what extent?

4.In order to determine the existence of a religious or linguistic minority in relation to Article 30, what is to be the unit-the State or the country as a whole?

5.To what extent can the rights of aided private minority institutions to administer be regulated?

• • •

CHAPTER XIX

P. A. I NAMDAR Vs. STATE OF MAHARASHTRA, 2004

Citations: (2004) 8 SCC 139

(BEFORE RUMA PAL AND ARUN KUMAR, JJ.)

SLPs (C) No. 9932 of 2004 with No. 9935 of 2004, WP No. 276 of 2004, SLPs (C) Nos. 10780 and 11244of2004 and IAs Nos. 22; 26-28,.30, 31,33 & in WP (C) No. 350 of 1993, decided on July 15,2004.

A·. Constitution of India -Arts. 19(1)(g) & (6), 30(1), 26(a)'and 15(4). -

Right to establish and administer educational institutions - Autonomy of private unaided, minority and non-minority professional colleges, Petitions raising issues relating to fixation of _admission quotas and, the holding of entrance examinations, all issues which related to interpretation of T.M.A. Pai case, (2002) 8 SCC· 481 and Islamic Academy case, (2003) SCC·697 -- Matter referred to a larger· Bench Interim orders given for the academic year-2004:.05 in ·respect of the fixation of admission quotas and entrance examinations ·

Islamic Academy of Educatio11 v . .. State of Karnataka. (2003) 6 sec 697;_ T.M.A. Pai Foundation v. State of Karnataka, (2002) 8 sec 481; Shahal H: Musaliar v. State of Kerala, (1993) 4 SCC 112; T.M.A. Pai Foundation v. State of Karnataka, (1993) 4 SCC 276; T.M.A. Pai Foundation v. State of Karnataka; (1994) 2 SCC 734; T.M.A. Pai

Foundation v. State of Karnataka, (1995) 5 SCC 220; T.M.A. Pai Fo1incta1io11 v. State Karnataka, (1996) 5 SCC 8; Medical Council of India v. Madhu Singh, (2002) 7, sec 258. referred to

B. Constitution of India -Arts. 19(1)(g) & (6), 30(1), 26(a).and 15(4)-

Words " their needs" occurring· in Islamic Academy case, (2003) 6 SCC·697, 6 , p. 730, para 19 (see para 6 herein)- Held, refer to the needs of the minority or non-minority unaided" professional college(s) and not the needs of -the State,

Islamic Academy of Education v. State of Karnataka. (2003) 6 SCC 697, clarified

C .. Constitution of-India -Arts. 19(1)(g) & (6), 30(1), 26(a) and 15(4) -

Exception to the rule in Islamic Academy case, (2003) 6 SCC 697 at p. 728, par 16 (see para 11 herein) granted in respect or those institutions which had their on admission procedure for 'the last twenty-five years _

Questions whether (a) tile restriction of 25 years would apply in all' case5, irrespective or the merits of the institutions or their background 'or' whether such a 1restriction was contrary to the decision 'in T.M.A. Pai: case, (2002) 8 SCC 481, (b) the decision in Islamic Academy in para 16, which limited the right a minority unaided professional institution to hold an entrance examination on its Own, was in the teeth of the pronouncement of the eleven Judge Bench decision in T.M.A. Pai in respect of the right of, the minority to evolve 'its work procedure and method for admission, (c) the clarification for certain phrases such as 'for example' and "particular type' occurring in the said para. 16 of Islamic Academy case, and (d) whether the decision in Islamic Academy did not cover a situation when there is only the one professional institution belonging to the minority, in which case it would not be in a position to form an association at all, left open.

• • •

CHAPTER XX

TECHNIP SA Vs. SMS HOLDING (PVT.) LTD. AND ORS. MAY 11, 2005

Citations: [2005] 1 Suppl. SCR 223, (2005) 5 SCC 465

[RUMA PAL, ARIJIT PASAYAT AND C.K. THAKKER, JJ.]

Securities and Exchange Board of India Act, 1992-Securities And Exchange Board of India (Substantial Acquisition of Shares and Takeover) Regulations, I 997-Regulations I 0, I I and I 2:

Acquisition of Indian Company, subsidiary of French Company by another French Company-Indian law/French law-Applicability of-Held:

Relationship of two French companies whether one of control or not is really a question of their status-The applicable law would, therefore be law of their domicile, namely, French law-However question as to their obligations under Indian law would have to be governed exclusively by Indian law.

Date of indirect acquisition-Determination of-S a subsidiary of C, a French company-T, another French company acquired C-T purchased 29.68% shares of C in April 2000-Shareholding of C in S did not constitute substantial part of assets of C-No evidence to show that T acquired C in April, 2000 to gain control of S- It was only a strategic alliance-Substantial acquisition took place in July 2001-Therefore date of acquisition is July 2001.

Words and phrases-'acquirer' and 'acting in concert '-Meaning of- In the context of Regulations 2(b) and 2(e) of Securities And Exchange Board of India (Substantial Acquisition of Shares and Takeover) Regulations, 1997.

Private International law: Foreign law-When not applicable-Held: Inapplicable when it is contrary to domestic public policy and morality.

Technip and Coflexip are French Companies. Seamec is an Indian Company and subsidiary of Coflexip. Technip acquired the control of Seamec through Coflexip. IFP and its subsidiary ISI are also French Government Companies. IFP was shareholder in Technip and Coflexip.

Dispute arose as to the date of acquisition. On complaint of Seamec shareholders before SEBI, it was held that French Law was applicable to the takeover for determining the date of acquisition. It found that Technip had Obtained control of Coflexip in July 2001 without Public offer. SEBI directed Technip to make public announcement as required under the Securities And Exchange Board of India (Substantial Acquisition of Shares and Takeover) Regulations, 1997 within 45 days and pay 15% interest to B shareholders for delayed announcement. Before Securities Appellate Tribunal (SAT), the grievance of Seamec shareholders was that date of control of Coflexip by Technip was April 2000 and not July 2001. Pending appeal, Technip made public announcement to acquire shares of Seamec by taking July 2001 as the relevant date. SAT however held that the relevant date was April 2000 as the applicable Jaw to the question was Indian Law and accordingly directed Technip to pay Seamec shareholders the difference between the price of shares between July 2001 and April 2000 together with 15% interest on such difference. One of the grounds on which SAT came to this conclusion that was based on the fact that both the companies had been promoted by IFP and that IFP through ISIS acting in concert with Technip had brought about the takeover of Coflexip by Technip. Hence the present appeal. A separate appeal is filed by IFP challenging the allegations made against it in SAT's order.

• • •

CHAPTER XXI

M/S. S.B.P. AND CO. Vs. M/S. PATEL ENGINEERING LTD. AND ANR. OCTOBER 26, 2005

Citations: [2005] 4 Suppl SCR 688, (2005) 8 SCC 618

[R.C. LAHOTI, CJ., B.N. AGRA WAL, ARUN KUMAR, G.P. MATHUR, A.K. MATHUR, P.K. BALASUBRAMANYAN AND C.K. THAKKER, JJ.]

Arbitration Act, 1940; Ss. 8, 20 and 21 The Arbitration and Conciliation Act, 1996; Ss. 2(h), 2(h), 7, 9, 11, 16 and 34/Code of Civil Procedure, 1908:

Functions performed by the Chief Justice of Supreme Court/Chief Justices of High Courts under Section 11 of the 1996 Act-Administrative or Judicial-Held: Judicial.

Held, Per majority: Once a statute creates an authority, confers on it powers to adjudicate and makes its decision final, the decision cannot be termed as purely administrative decision-The ground of ensuring minimum judicial interference by itself is not a ground to hold the power so conferred is only an administrative power-When the power is conferred so as to decide on the existence of the conditions justifying appointment of an arbitrator/arbitral tribunal and is conferred on judicial authority/Chief Justice unless shown otherwise, the Chief Justice has to act judicially-When Chief Justice is called upon to decide on the existence of arbitration agreement/appointment of arbitrator/constitution of tribunal and confronted with two different point of view contended for by the rival parties in deciding so he cannot be said to be performing administrative function-Issuance of Notice to opposite party cannot be construed to be merely an intimation but it really gives an opportunity of being heard-Since the Chief Justice has necessarily to apply his mind before coming to a conclusion to appoint/not to appoint an arbitrator, the decision so arrived at could appropriately be termed as judicial decision.

Chief Justice exercising power to appoint an arbitrator/constitute arbitral tribunal-Interference by the tribunal-Held: Tribunal cannot go behind the decision of the Chief Justice and rule on its own jurisdiction. Conferment of power on Chief Justice to appoint an arbitrator Characteristics of-Held: It cannot be termed as persona designata as it is conferred on a class and not on an individual-Since the intention of the legislature is to entrust the power to the highest judicial authorities in the State/country, the Chief Justice could designate other judge of the same Court but he cannot designate a District Judge to perform the functions in terms of Section 11, sub-section (6) of the Act.

Order of the arbitral tribunal-Challenge under Article 226/227 of the Constitution-Held: Not permissible.

Words and Phrases: 'Court '-Meaning of Held per minority:

When an appropriate authority after applying its mind in terms of the circumstances enumerated in the Act arrived at a decision, the decision cannot be considered on that basis as judicial/quasi-judicial and not administrative-The Chief Justice arrives at a decision of appointing an arbitrator after satisfying itself to the existence of an arbitration agreement and failure on the part of one of the parties to approve appointment of an arbitrator-Such decision is merely of prima facie in nature and by passing such order he does not decide lis nor contentious issues between the parties Thus performing of such functions does not make the function of the Chief Justice as judicial/quasi judicial-The power to appoint an arbitrator is given to the Chief Justice to ensure fairness, integrity and impartiality but that does not mean that the Chief Justice is exercising judicial/quasi-judicial powers-By appointing an arbitrator, the Chief Justice is performing administrative functions, as he is not under the obligation to act judicially But he is under obligation/duty to act fairly and therefore requires to issue notice to other party before taking a decision to appoint an arbitrator-Constitution of India, 1950-Articles 226 and 227.

Power of Chief Justice-Delegation-Held: Not permissible.

• • •

CHAPTER XXII

RAMESHWAR PRASAD AND ORS. Vs. UNION OF INDIA AND ANR. JANUARY 24, 2006

Citations: [2006] 1 SCR 562, (2006) 2 SCC 1

[Y.K. SABHARWAL, CJ., K.G. BALAKRISHNAN, B.N. AGRAWAL, ASHOK BHAN AND ARIJIT PASAYAT, JJ.)

Constitution of India, 1950; Articles 32/226, 356, 74 and 163:

Invoking of power under Article 356-Issue of proclamation-- Subjective satisfaction of President-Conditions precedent-Scope of judicial review.

Articles 356 and 74-Satisfaction of President under - Nature of Duty of Council of Ministers before recommending issuance of proclamation- -On facts, held: Governor has misled Union Council of Ministers.

Article 356--Nature and Scope of power---Held, is an emergency power but not an absolute power.

Articles 32, 226 and Preamble-Scope of interference.

Articles 356, 163 and 174(2)(b)-Dissolution of State Assembly-Floor test-Necessity of.

Articles 356, I74(2)(b), 85(2)(b) and Schedule X-Dissolution of newly elected Assembly-Grounds to be taken into consideration-Hung Assembly---Realignment of parties/MLAs-Unethical means/horse riding Recommendation of dissolution on that ground-Scope of judicial review in such situations.

Articles 159, 163, 164, I 74(2)(b) and 356--Installation of new Government after election-Duty of Governor.

Articles 79, 168, 245 and 246-Parliament-Nature of acts of -When legislative.

Articles 356, 174(2)(b). 85, 32 and 226-Unconstitutionality of proclamation under Article 356 dissolving Legislative Assembly of State power to mould relief Articles 157 and 155-Governor-Criteria for appointment of-Suggestions given in Sarkaria Commission Report-Need for observance of Articles 163, 153, 154 and 159-Governor-Nature and role of office of-Discharge of powers and duties-Discretionary powers-Scope of Article 361-Scope of immunity granted to Governors and President Discussed.

Articles 327, 324, 329, 174, 168, 172, 83. 85 and 79-"Due constitution" or coming into existence of a. legislative Assembly-When takes place.

Words and Phrases:

"Emergency "-Meaning of in the context of Part XVlll of the Constitution.

"Merger"-Meaning of in the context of Para 4 Schedule X of the Constitution.

"Required"-Meaning of in the context of discretionary powers of the Governor under the Constitution.

In these Writ Petitions, the petitioners have challenged the validity of the proclamation dated 23rd May, 2005 issued under Article 356 of the Constitution ordering dissolution of Bihar Legislative Assembly. They have also prayed for restoration of the Election Commission Notification dated 4th March, 2005 issued under Section 73 of the Representation of People Act, 1951 notifying the names of the elected members.

It was contended on behalf of the petitioners that the allegations in the Governor's report of horse trading was factually incorrect and fictional. It was incumbent upon the Governor to verify the facts personally from the MLAs; that under the scheme of the Constitution the decision with regard to mergers and disqualifications on the ground of defection or horse trading is vested in the Speaker; and that the Governor could not have attempted to act on that basis and arrogated to himself such an authority. Relying heavily on the Nine Judge Bench judgment of this Court in S.R .. Bommai and Ors. v. Union of India and Ors .. [1994] 3 SCC I, it was contended that action of the Governor is malafide in law; irrational, without any cogent material to support the conclusion arrived at and is based on mere ipse dixit and, thus, was not sustainable in law. It was contended that in exercise of judicial review this Court should quash the impugned notification and as a consequence restore the legislative assembly constituted by the Election Commission notification dated 4th March, 2005.

It was further contended that before even elected candidates making and subscribing oath or affirmation, as contemplated by Article 188 of the Constitution, even the Assembly could not be placed under suspended animation and status quo as on the date of issue of notification under Section 73 of the RP Act of 1951 deserves to be directed.

After hearing arguments on the question of the Governor not being answerable to any Court in view of immunity granted by Article 361(1) of the Constitution, this Court accepted the submission of the Government that notice may not be issued to the Governor, and for giving brief reason in the order to be followed by detailed reasons later.

The points that fell for determination by this Court are :

(1) Is it permissible to dissolve the Legislative Assembly under Article 174(2)(b) of the Constitution without its first meeting taking place?

(2) Whether the proclamation dated 23rd May, 2005 dissolving the Assembly of Bihar is illegal and unconstitutional?

(3) If the answer to the aforesaid question is in affirmative, is it necessary to direct status quo ante as on 7th March, 2005 or 4th March, 2005?

(4) What is the scope of Article 361 granting immunity to the Governor?

After hearing elaborate arguments, by a brief order dated 7th October, 2005, the notification dated 23rd May, 2005 was held to be unconstitutional but having regard to the facts and circumstances of the case, relief directing status quo ante to restore the Legislative Assembly as it stood on 7th March, 2005, was declined.

• • •

CHAPTER XXIII

LR. COELHO (DEAD) BY LRS. V. STATE OF TAMIL NADU, JANUARY I I, 2007

Citations: [2007] 1 SCR 706, (2007) 2 SCC 1

(Y.K. SABHARWAL CJI, ASHOK BHAN, DR. ARIJIT PASAYAT, B.P. SINGH, S.H. KAPADIA, C.K. THAKKER, P.K. BALASUBRAMANYAN, ALTAMAS KABIR AND D.K. JAIN, JJ.]

Constitution of India, 1950: Article 368 read with Article 31-B, Article 32-Ninth Schedule Amendment of Constitution-Inclusion of enactments in Ninth Schedule Judicial review of-Held: a law that abrogates or abridges rights guaranteed by Part Ill of the Constitution and also violates the basic structure doctrine, whether by amendment of any Article of Part Ill or by an insertion in Ninth Schedule, such law will have to be invalidated in exercise of power of judicial review of the Court-All amendments to the Constitution made on or after 24.4.1973 by which Ninth Schedule is amended by inclusion of various laws therein can be tested on the touchstone of basic or essential features of Constitution as reflected in Article 21 read with Articles 14 and 19 and the principles underlying them by application of the "right test" and the "essence of the right test"-While laws may be added to the Ninth Schedule, once Article 32 is resorted to the legislation concerned must answer to the complete test of fundamental rights-Article 31-B after 24.4.1973, despite its wide language, cannot confer unlimited or unregulated immunity- If infraction affects the basic structure, such a law will not get protection of Ninth Schedule -Saving-If validity of any.

Ninth Schedule law has already been upheld by Supreme Court, it would not be open to challenge again on principles declared in this judgment Action taken and transactions finalized as a result of impugned Acts shall not be open to challenge-

Constitutionalism-Doctrine of separation of powers-Doctrine of basic structure--Judicial review.

Constitutionalism-Constitution of India-Doctrine of basic structure-Held, equality, rule of law, judicial review, separation of powers, secularism, reasonable balance between Fundamental Rights and Directive Principles, form part of the basic structure-Each of these concepts are intimately connected-

After enunciation of the basic structure doctrine, full judicial review is an integral part of the constitutional scheme Constitution of India- Articles 14,15,16,19,20,21and 32.

Interpretation of Constitution-Constitutional provisions have to be construed having regard to the march of time and the development of law- Abrogation and abridgement of fundamental rights, therefore, have to be examined on broad interpretation.

On the Gudalur Janmam Estates (Abolition and Conversion into Ryotwari) Act, 1969 having been struck down by the Supreme Court, and section 2(c) of the West Bengal Land Holding Revenue Act, 1979 having been struck down by the Calcutta High Court, and the Supreme Court having dismissed the consequential special leave petition filed by the State Government, the Parliament, by the Constitution (Thirty-Fourth Amendment) Act, inserted the Janmam Act in the Ninth Schedule to the Constitution of India and, by the Constitution Sixty-sixth Amendment) Act, inserted the West Bengal Land Holding Revenue Act, 1979 in the Ninth Schedule.

These insertions were challenged before a Constitution Bench of the Supreme Court The said Constitution Bench was of the opinion that the decision in Waman Rao and Ors. v. Union of India and Ors., (1981) 2 SC 3623 to the effect that amendments to the Constitution on or after 24th April 1973 (i.e. the date of decision in His Holiness Kesavananda Bharti Sripadagulvaru v. State of Kerala and Anr., [1973] 4 SCC 225 by which the Ninth Schedule was amended from time to time by inclusion of various Acts and, regulations therein, were open to challenge on the ground that they, or anyone or more of them, were beyond the constituent power of Parliament since they damage the basic or essential features of the Constitution or its basic structure, would need reconsideration by a larger Bench preferably of nine Judges. Thus, the matter was placed before the present nine-Judge Bench.

On the questions: whether on and after 24th April, 1973 when basic structure doctrine was propounded, it is permissible for the Parliament under Article 31B to immunize legislations from fundamental rights by inserting them into the Ninth Schedule and, if so, what is its effect on the power of judicial review of the Court; and what is the extent and nature of immunity that Article 31-B can provide.

• • •

CHAPTER XXIV

COMMON CAUSE (A REGO. SOCIETY) v. UNION OF INDIA & ORS. APRIL 11, 2008.

Citations: [2008] 6 SCR 262, (2008) 5 SCC 511

(H.K. SEMA AND MARKANDEY KATJU, JJ.)

Public Interest Litigation - Petitioner seeking directions to authorities for taking various traffic safety measures to control occurrence of road accidents - Scope of - Held: Futile reactions to authorities as sought for by the petitioner amounts to legislative/executive action, which only the legislature/executive is competent to give - Judiciary cannot encroach into the domain of the legislature/executive - The Courts must exercise judicial restraint and must not perform executive.

legislative functions - Article 21 of the Constitution must not be used by the Courts to justify very kind of direction/grant every kind of claim- Not only should the Court not to give such directions because that would violate the principles of separations power but also because these are highly technical matters to be dealt with by the experts - Judiciary has its limits ad cannot solve all the problems - The country can ill-afford t be governed through court decrees - Moreover, adequate provisions available under Motor Vehicles Act for controlling the traffic and are obviously meant for road safety - Also there exists a Road Safety Council which has been suggesting measures for road safety - If further provisions are required, the petitioner may approach the legislature/executive - It is clarified that the Court can certainly not amend the law – Motor Vehicles Act, 1988 – Constitution of India, 1950 - Articles 14 and 21 - Judicial restraint - Exercise of Judicial activism - Legitimate/illegitimate - Held: Courts giving wider meaning to Articles 14 and 21 of the Constitution, in the light of new developments in the country, amounts to legitimate exercise of power - However, Courts laying down new principles of law specifically reserved for the legislature amounts to illegitimate exercise of judicial power. Adjudication - Held: It must be done within the system of historically validated restraints and conscious minimization of Judges preferences.

Judicial activism - Scope of - Discussed.

Doctrines:

Doctrine of 'Separation of powers' - Applicability of.

Petitioner is a registered society which claims to be engaged in espousing problems of general public importance. A writ petition has been field by the petitioner before this Court highlighting various problems connected with traffic and road safety measures. In o connection thereof, the petitioner sought for issuing appropriate directions to the respondents and others for taking steps to set up fully satisfactory procedures of licensing of vehicles, licensing of drivers and to impart proper training required in connection thereto; to ensure to provide requisite infrastructure on ·roads in order to maintain discipline on roads viz. signs, signals, footpaths, repair of roads etc. to ensure the availability of ambulances for immediate shifting of injured to the hospitals; to set up Expert Committees to suggest for minimizing the road accidents; and to take further steps for improvement of the overall traffic system.

• • •

CHAPTER XXV

STATE OF WEST BENGAL & ORS. Vs. THE COMMITTEE FOR PROTECTION OF DEMOCRATIC RIGHTS, WEST BENGAL & ORS. FEBRUARY 17, 2010

Citations: [2010] 2 SCR 979, (2010) 3 SCC 571

[K.G. BALAKRISHNAN, CJI., R.V. RAVEENDRAN, D.K. JAIN, P. SATHASIVAM AND J.M. PANCHAL, JJ.]

Constitution of India, 1950: Articles 32 and 226 Article 21 - Fundamental rights - Fair and impartial investigation - Judicial Review - Direction by Supreme Court/High Court to CBI to investigate a cognizable offence committed within territorial jurisdiction of a State without the consent of the State Government -

HELD: Will neither impinge upon the federal structure of the Constitution nor will it violate the doctrine of separation of powers, and shall be valid in law - State has a duty to enforce · human rights of a citizen providing for fair and impartial investigation - Constitutional courts can exercise its power of judicial review and direct CBI to take up investigation within the jurisdiction of the State - However, this extra ordinary power must be exercised sparingly, cautiously and in exceptional situations only when the Court after considering the material on record ·comes to a conclusion that such material does disclose a prima facie case calling for an investigation by CBI or any other similar agency – Restriction on Parliament by the Constitution and on the Executive by Parliament under an enactment do not amount to restriction on power of Judiciary under Articles 32 and 226 - The restriction imposed by s. 6 of the Special Police Act on the powers of the Union, cannot be read as restriction on the powers of the constitutional courts - Delhi Special Police Establishment Act, 1946, ss. 3, 5 and 6 - Investigation. Articles 13, 32, 142, 144 and 226 - Judicial Review - Nature and scope of - HELD: The Constitution expressly confers the power of judicial review on the Supreme Court and : High Courts under Articles 32 and 226 respectively - In view of the constitutional scheme and the jurisdiction conferred on the Supreme Court under Article 32 and on High Courts under Article 226, the power of judicial review being an integral part and essential feature of the Constitution constituting its basic structure, no Act of Parliament can exclude or curtail the powers of the constitutional courts with regard to the enforcement of fundamental rights - Besides supremacy of the Constitution, separation of powers between Legislature, - Executive and Judiciary constitutes basic feature of the · Constitution - Nevertheless, judicial review stands entirely on a different pedestal - Judicial review is essential for resolving the disputes regarding the limits of constitutional power and entering the constitutional limitations as an ultimate interpreter of the Constitution - Judicial review of laws is embedded in the Constitution by virtue of Article 13 read with Articles 32 and 226 of the Constitution - It acts as the final arbiter not only to give effect to the distribution of legislative powers between the Parliament and the State Legislatures, it is also necessary to show any transgression by each entity - Significance of and difference between power of Supreme Court under Articles 32, 142 and 144 and that of High Court under Article 226 - Explained - Doctrines - Separation of powers - Basic structure theory-Principle of constitutionality.

Articles 245 and 246 r/w Seventh Schedule, List I, Entries 2-A and 80 - List II, Entry 2, List Ill and Articles 32 and 226 - Legislative powers of Parliament and State Legislatures -Judicial review of- HELD: The broad proposition is that under the Constitution there is a clear demarcation of legislative powers between the Union and the States and they have to confine themselves within the field entrusted to them -

However, the words "notwithstanding anything contained in clauses (2) and (3)" in Article 246

(1) and the words subject to clauses (1) and (2) in Article 246 (3) lay down the principle of federal supremacy viz. that in case of inevitable conflict between Union and State powers, the Union power as enumerated in List I shall prevail over the State power as enumerated in Lists II and Ill and in case of an overlapping between Lists II and Ill, the latter shall prevail - But, the principle of federal supremacy laid down in Article 246 cannot be resorted to unless there is an irreconcilable direct conflict between the entries in the Union and the State Lists - If the federal structure is violated by any legislative action, the Constitution takes care to protect the federal structure by ensuring that Courts act as guardians and interpreters of the Constitution and provide remedy under Articles 32 and 226, whenever there is an attempted violation - Doctrine of separation of powers.

In the instant appeals and writ petitions, the question referred for consideration of the Constitution Bench was:

whether the High Court, in exercise of its jurisdiction under Article 226 of the Constitution of India, could direct the Central Bureau of Investigation, established under the Delhi Special Police Establishment Act, 1946, to investigate a cognizable offence, which was alleged to have taken place within the territorial jurisdiction of a State, without the consent of the State Government.

• • •

CHAPTER XXVI

SMT. SELVI & ORS. Vs. STATE OF KARNATAKA. MAY 5, 2007

Citations: [2010] 5 SCR 381, (2010) 7 SCC 263

[K.G. BALAKRISHNAN, CJI., R.V. RAVEENDRAN ANDJ.M. PANCHAL, JJ.]

CODE OF CRIMINAL PROCEDURE, 1973:

Section 161 (2), Explanation to Sections 53, 53-A and 54 - Investigation - Examination of accused persons, suspects and witnesses - Use of certain scientific techniques viz. narcoanalysis, polygraph examination and Brain Electrical Activation Profile (BEAP) test - Involuntary administration of - Held: Violative of Article 20(3) of the Constitution of India -

However, any information or material that is subsequently discovered with the help of voluntary administered test results can be admitted in accordance with Section 27 of Evidence Act - Guidelines formulated by National Human Rights Commission to be strictly adhered to - Similar safeguards should be adopted for conducting such tests – Constitution of India, 1950, Article 20(3)- Evidence Act, 1872, Section 27, Criminal Investigation - Video recordings of narcoanalysis interviews - Leakage to media by the investigation agency - A worrisome practice since public distribution of these recordings can expose the subject to undue social stigma and specific risks - May even encourage vigilantism in addition to media trial.

CONSTITUTION OF INDIA, 1950:

Article 20(3) - Right against self-incrimination - Polygraph examination and Brain Electrical Activation Profile (BEAP) test - Results obtained from these tests should be treated as 'personal testimony' since they are a means for 'imparting personal knowledge about relevant facts' - Hence, the results obtained through involuntary administration of either of the impugned tests viz. narcoanalysis technique,

polygraph examination and BEAP test comes within the scope of testimonial compulsion thereby attracting the protective shield of Article 20(3).

Article 21 - Personal liberty - Involuntary administration of narcoanalysis technique, polygraph examination and BEAP Test - Whether a reasonable restriction or personal liberty - Held: No person should be forcibly subjected to any of the abovesaid techniques whether in the context of investigation in criminal cases or otherwise - Doing so would amount to unwarranted intrusion into personal liberty.

The legal questions in the batch of criminal appeals relate to the involuntary administration of certain scientific techniques, namely narcoanalysis, polygraph examination and the Brain Electrical Activation Profile (BEAP) test for the purpose of improving investigation efforts in criminal cases. The involuntary administration of the impugned techniques evoked questions about the protective scope of the 'right against self-incrimination' which finds place in Article 20(3) of the Constitution. Arguments were advanced invoking the guarantee of 'substantive due process' which is part and parcel of the idea of 'personal liberty' protected by Article 21 of the Constitution. The main question raised in this regard was whether the provisions in the Code of Criminal Procedure, 1973 that provide for 'medical examination' during the course of investigation can be read expansively to include the impugned techniques, even though the latter are not explicitly enumerated. Questions have also been raised with respect to the professional. ethics of medical personnel involved in the administration of these techniques. Furthermore, Article 21 has been judicially expanded to include a 'right against cruel, inhuman or degrading treatment', requiring this Court to determine whether the involuntary administration of the impugned techniques violates this right whose scope corresponds with evolving international human rights norms. Contentions were raised invoking the test subject's 'right to privacy', both in a physical and mental sense. On the basis of the issues involved and contentions raised, the Court framed the following questions:

I. Whether the involuntary administration of the impugned techniques violate the 'right against self-incrimination' enumerated in Article 20(3) of the Constitution?

1-A. Whether the investigative use of the impugned techniques creates a likelihood of incrimination for the subject?

1-B. Whether the results derived from the impugned techniques amount to 'testimonial compulsion' thereby attracting the bar of Article 20(3)?

II, Whether the involuntary administration of the impugned techniques is a reasonable restriction on F

'personal liberty' as understood in the context of Article 21 of the Constitution?

• • •

CHAPTER XXVII

RE: SPECIAL REFERENCE No.1 OF 2012 [Under Article 143(1) of the Constitution of India] SEPTEMBER 27, 2012

Citations: [2012] 9 SCR 311, (2012) 10 SCC 1

[S.H. KAPADIA, CJI, D.K. JAIN, JAGDISH SINGH KHEHAR, DIPAK MISRA AND RANJAN GOGOI, JJ.)

CONSTITUTION OF INOIA, 1950:

Art 143(1) - Power of President to consult Supreme Court- Scope of - It is not necessary that the question on which the opinion of Supreme Court is sought must have actually arisen - The President can make a reference even at an anterior stage, namely, at the stage when the President is satisfied that the question is likely to arise - The satisfaction whether the question meets pre-requisites of Art. 143(1) is essentially a matter for the President to decide - Upon receipt of a reference under Art. 143(1), the only discretion Supreme Court has is either to answer the reference or respectfully decline to send a report to the President - In the instant Reference, Question no. 1 involves interpretation of a constitutional principle inherent under Art. 14 of the Constitution and it is of great public importance as it deals with allocation/alienation/ disposal/ distribution of natural resources. Art. 137 and 143(1) - Review and Reference – Difference between - Explained - Held: Merely because a review of the judgment of Supreme Court in a case had been filed and withdrawn and in the recital of Reference, the narration pertains to the said case, the same would not be an embargo or impediment for exercise of discretion to answer the Reference.

Art. 143 (1) - Presidential Reference - Notice – Practice and procedure.

Art. 143(1) - Presidential Reference subsequent to decision of Supreme Court in "2G Case" - Maintainability of - Held: The Reference is maintainable, notwithstanding its effect on the ratio of 2G Case, as long as the decision in that case qua tis inter partes is left unaffected - By the Reference, Court's opinion is sought on the limited point of permissibility of methods other than auction for alienation of natural resources, other than spectrum - It has been stated on behalf of Government of India that it is not questioning the correctness of directions in 2G Case, in so far as a/

location of spectrum is concerned and, in fact, Government is in the process of implementing the same, in letter and spirit - As long as the decision with respect to allocation of spectrum licenses is untouched, the Court is within its jurisdiction to evaluate and clarify ratio of the judgment in 2G Case.

• • •

CHAPTER XXVIII

REPUBLIC OF ITALY AND ORS. Vs. UNION OF INDIA AND ORS. JANUARY 18, 2013

Citations: [2013] 4 SCR 595, (2013) 4 SCC 721

[ALTAMAS KABIR, CJI AND J. CHELAMESWAR, JJ.]

International Law:

Incident of firing at a distance of about 20. 5 nautical miles from the Indian sea-coast of the State of Kerala - Firing by officers of naval staff of Italy deployed on merchant ship of Italy - Resulting in death of two persons on Indian Fishing Vessel - FIR against two officers u/s. 302/34 IPC lodged in the State of Kerala - State Police investigated the matter and arrested the accused - Writ Petition u/Art. 226 of the Constitution by the accused challenging the jurisdiction of State of Kerala in registering FIR, in investigating the matter and in arresting the accused - During pendency of the writ petition criminal proceedings were also initiated against the accused in Italy under Italian Penal Code - The Consul General of Italy asserted that Italy had exclusive jurisdiction over the accused and they· having acted in official capacity were entitled to sovereign and functional immunity – During pendency of the judgment of High Court, Republic of Italy invoked jurisdiction u/Art. 32 of the Constitution for the same reliefs - As the writ petition u/Art. 226 was dismissed, SLP also filed - HELD: Action by State o' Kerala was without jurisdiction because the incident took place within Contiguous Zone on which the State did not have jurisdiction - Also because in the case, two sovereign countries were involved and one country had already initiated criminal proceedings against the accused, State of Kerala as one of the units of the federal unit would not have authority to try the accused - 'Declaration on Principles of International Law Concerning Family Relations and Co-operation between States in accordance with the Charters of United Nations' has to be conducted at federal level and not at provincial level - The incident cannot be said to be an "incident of navigation" within the meaning of Art. 97 of UNCLOS - By virtue of extension of the provisions of IPC and Cr. P. C. to contiguous zone, Union of India is 1mtitled to take cognizance, investigate and try the accused - But the same is subject to the provisions of Art. 100 of UNCLOS -

Direction to Union of India to set up Special Court to try the case - Accused can also invoke provisions of Article 100 of UNCLOS whereupon the question of jurisdiction to investigate into the incident and for the courts in India to try the accused would be considered - If found that both the countries i.e. India as well as Italy have concurrent jurisdiction over the matter, the directions passed in this judgment will continue – Penal Code, 1860 - ss. 302, 307, 427 r/w s.34 - Suppression of Unlawful Acts Against Safety of Maritime Navigation and Fixed Platforms on Continental Shelf Act, 2002 - s.3 – United Nations Convention on the Law of the Sea, 1982 – Articles 97and 100 - Maritime Zones Act, 1976 - Declaration on Principles of International Law Concerning Family Relations and Co-operation Between States in accordance with the Charters of United Nations - Constitution of India, 1950 – Article 297.

Petitioner Nos. 2 and 3 and four other officers of naval staff of Republic of Italy were deployed in the board of merchant ship which was flying the Italian Flag. The deployment was pursuant to a Government decree of Republic of Italy, which was enacted to protect the Italian ships from piracy in international seas. At a distance of about 20.5 nautical miles from the Indian Sea-Coast, off the State of Kerala, the Italian ships mistook an Indian Fishing Vessel to be a pirate vessel and opened fire on it. Two persons of the Indian Fishing Vessel were killed on account of the firing. FIR was lodged uls. 302/34 IPC at the Police Station in the State of Kerala.

The Republic of Italy filed a writ petition challenging the jurisdiction of the State of Kera la and that of the State Police to register the FIR and to conduct investigation and to arrest them. They prayed for quashing the FIR as being without jurisdiction, contrary to law, null and void.

The High Court reserved the judgment. In the meantime, the petitioners filed Writ Petition before this Court, asking for the same reliefs. During pendency of the Writ Petition u/Art. 32, the State Police filed charge-sheet against petitioner Nos. 2 and 3 u/ss. 302, 307, 427 r/w. s. 34 IPC and u/s. 3 of the Suppression of Unlawful Acts Against Safety of Maritime Navigation and Fixed Platforms on Continental Shelf Act, 2002. When the High Court dismissed the Writ Petition, Special Leave Petition was filed before this Court.

Primarily it was contended on behalf of petitioner Nos. 2 and 3 that the State Police had no jurisdiction to investigate the incident; that in view of public international law, the Courts of the Republic of Italy had jurisdiction to try the accused and not the Indian Courts, because the incident occurred beyond the territory of India to which location sovereignty of India did not extend; that Parliament cannot extend the application of the laws enacted by it, beyond the territory of India; that the incident which resulted in the death of two Indians was an 'incident of navigation' within the meaning of Article 97 of the United Nations Convention on the Law of the Sea (UNCLOS).

• • •

CHAPTER XXIX

NOVARTIS AG Vs. UNION OF INDIA & OTHERS. APRIL 01, 2013

Citations: [2013] 13 SCR 148, (2013) 6 SCC 1

[AFTAB ALAM AND RANJANA PRAKASH DESAI, JJ.)

Patents Act, 1970:

c ss. 2(1)(j), 2(1)(ja) and 3(d) - Grant of patent - To lmatinib Mesylate in Beta Crystalline form - Twin test of "Invention" and "patentability" - Held: The patent product fails in both the tests of 'invention' and 'patentability' - It is a known substance of Zimmermann patent - It is not a new product - Not only is lmatinib Mesylate known as substance of Zimmermann but its pharmacological properties are known in the Zimmermann patent - It does not qualify the test of invention as laid down in s.2(1)(j) and 2(1)(ja) - lmatinib Mesylate is known substance with known efficacy – Thus BETA Crystalline form of lmatinib Mesylate is a new form of known substance - It fully attracts s.3(d} - The higher solubility that is attributed to the beta crystalline form of lmatinib Mesylate would be limited to (i) More beneficial flow properties, (ii) Better thermodynamic stability, and (iii) Lower Hygroscopicity- These properties, "physical attributes" would give the subject product improved processability and better and longer storability but, on the basis of those properties alone, the beta crystalline form of lmatinib Mesylate certainly cannot be said to possess enhanced efficacy over lmatinib Mesylate, the known substance immediately preceding it, within the meaning of s. 3(d) of the. Act. s.2(1)(j), (ac), (ja) - Invention - Held: In order to qualify - as 'invention' a product must satisfy the test i.e. it must be new, it must be capable of being made or used in the industry and it must come into being as a result of an invention which has a feature that entails technical advance over existing knowledge or has an economic significance and makes the invention not obvious to a person skilled in the art. s.2(1) ()) - Invention - Chemicals and pharmaceuticals - Held: A new product in chemicals and especially pharmaceutical may. not necessarily mean something altogether new or completely unfamiliar or not existing before. s.3(d) - Test of Efficacy - Held: Depends upon the function, utility or the purpose of product under consideration - Test of enhanced efficacy in case of chemical substance, especially medicine, should receive narrow and strict interpretation. s.3(d) - Mere change of form with properties inherent to that form, would not qualify as "enhancement of efficacy" of a known substance.

Words and Phrases - 'Efficacy' - Meaning of, in the context of Patents Act, 1970.

The appellant in appeal Nos. 2706-2716 of 2013 filed application before Patent Office for grant of patent for lmatinib Mesylate in Beta Crystalline form. The application was made on July 17, 1998 giving July 18, 1997, the date on which the appellant had applied for grant of patent for the subject product in Switzerland as the 'priority date".

The application of the appellant lay dormant under an arrangement called 'Mailbox Procedure'. In 2003, the appellant was granted Exclusive Marketing Rights for the subject product. The application for patent was taken out of the 'Mailbox' after the amendments were made in the Patents Act, 1970, w.e.f. January 1,· 2005. Five pregrant oppositions were filed against the patent application of the appellant.

The application of the appellant was rejected on the grounds viz. the invention claimed, was anticipated by ;prior publication i.e. Zimmerman patent; that the invention claimed, was obvious to a person skulked in the art, in view of the disclosure provided in the Zimmerman patent specifications; that patentability of the claimed invention was disallowed by s. 3(d); and that the Swiss priority date i.e. July 17, 1997 was wrongly claimed as priority date for the application in India and hence the invention was also anticipated by the specification made yc in the application submitted in Switzerland. The appellant challenged the orders before High Court which was later transferred to Intellectual Property Appellate Board. The appeals were dismissed by the Board on the ground that -patentability of the subject product was hit by s. 3(d) as well as 3(b).

One of the appellants had also filed writ petitions seeking a declaration that. 3(d) of the Patents Act was unconstitutional being violative of Art. 14 and being not in compliance with Trade Related Aspects of Intellectual Property Rights (TRIPS). The petitions were dismissed by the High Court.

The appellant directly approached the Supreme Court u/Art. 136 of the Constitution against the order of Appellate. Board Dismissing the appeal of the appellant-applicant and allowing those filed by the objectors, the Court.

• • •

CHAPTER XXX

DR. BALRAM PRASAD Vs. DR. KUNAL SAHA & ORS. OCTOBER 24, 2013

Citations: [2013] 12 SCR 30, (2014) 1 SCC 384

[CHANDRAMAULI KR. PRASAD AND V. GOPALA GOWDA, JJ.]

CONSUMER PROTECTION ACT, 1986:

Complaint - Medical negligence - Contributory negligence - Death of an US based patient in hospital in India- National Commission holding the hospital and doctors liable for medical negligence as also the husband of deceased liable for contributory negligence and, as such, deducting 10% towards contributory negligence from compensation, awarding Rs. 1,55,58,750 to claimant - Held: Appellant-Hospital is vicariously liable for its doctors and is, therefore, directed to pay total amount of compensation amounting to Rs. 6, 08, 00, 5501-, under various heads as detailed in judgment, after deducting Rs.25 lakhs payable by appellants doctors - National Commission erred in holding that claimant had contributed to negligence of appellant-doctors and Hospital which resulted in death of his wife when Supreme Court had clearly absolved the claimant of such liability and remanded the matter back to National Commission only for determining the quantum of compensation - Finding of National Commission in this regard is set aside and it is reemphasized that claimant did not contribute to negligence of appellants-doctors and Hospital which resulted in death of his wife - Consumer Protection Rules, 1987 -r4(c).

Enhancement of compensation by complainant subsequent to filing of claim petition - Claimant making additional claims by way of affidavit before National Commission - Held: Claim for enhancement of compensation by claimant is justified - Claimant is entitled for enhanced compensation under certain items in additional claim preferred before National Commission - Further, claim of claimant having remained pending for 15 years, value of money has devalued to a great extent - Therefore, inflation should be considered while deciding the quantum of compensation - It is wholly untenable in law for the 'Hospital and the doctors to plead that without there being an amendment to the claim petition, the claimant is not entitled to seek the additional claims by way of affidavit, and that the claim is barred by limitation -- Supreme Court has got the power under Art. 136 of the Constitution and the duty to award just and reasonable compensation to do complete justice to the affected claimant - Code of Civil Procedure, 1908 - Constitution of India, 1950 - Art. 136. Just and fair compensation - Held: Status, future prospects and educational qualification of deceased must be judged for deciding adequate, just and fair compensation - Principle of just and reasonable compensation is based on 'restitution tegrum', i.e., claimant must receive the sum of money which would put him in the same position as he would have been if he had not sustained the wrong - Court is duty bound and entitled to award just compensation' irrespective of the fact whether any plea in that behalf was raised by claimant or not. Future prospects of income - Held, 'Future loss of income' is different from 'future prospects of income' in terms of potential of victim - Jn awarding just and reasonable compensation, future prospects of deceased must have been reasonably judged by the National Commission. Medical negligence - Compensation - Multiplier method Held: Just, fair and reasonable compensation has to be determined on the basis of the income of accessed at the time of death of the victim and other related claims on account of the death - Therefore, the plea to apply tile multiplier method in determination of compensation, does not inspire confidence.

Medical negligence - Death of patient – Compensation towards loss of income of deceased - Held: While determining the income of deceased, evidence on record has to be relied on - Further, 30% added towards future loss of income of deceased - 113 of total income is required to be deducted towards personal expenditure of deceased -

Estimating the life expectancy of a healthy person as 70 years, compensation to be awarded by multiplying the total loss of income by 30.

Medical negligence - Death of patient - Claim by husband under the heads loss of income for missed work, travel expenses and legal expenses - Held: Claim towards missed work cannot be allowed as the same has no direct nexus with the negligence of appellant-doctors and hospital -

However, claim towards travel expenses and legal expenses, partly allowed.

Other pecuniary damages - Medical negligence – Death of patient -- Expenses incurred by claimant towards treatment, travel and hotel expenses in this regard, allowed.

Non-pecuniary damages -Medical negligence - Death of patient -- Compensation under the head) Jain and suffering of patient during the course of treatment', allowed - Loss of consortium, allowed -- However, under the head, 'emotional distress, pain and suffering for claimant himself', no compensation can be awarded since this cl;3im bears no direct link with negligence of hospital and doctors in treating claimant's wife.

Medical negligence - Interest on compensation amount - Held: Not awarding interest by National Commission on compensation amount from the date of filing of original complaint up to the date of payment is most unreasonable and is opposed to provisions of Interest Act - Therefore, 6% interest is awarded on the compensation finally determined from date of the petition till payment - Interest Act, 1978.

Medical Negligence -- Liability of nursing homes, hospitals and doctors - Need of an appropriate legislation - Held: Doctors, hospitals and nursing homes and other connected establishments are required to be dealt with strictly if they are found to be negligent with patients and do not take their responsibility seriously - Central and State Governments may consider enacting laws wherever there is absence of one, for effective functioning of private hospitals and nursing homes.

The wife of the claimant-respondent no. 1 (C.A. No. 692/2012) died while she was undergoing treatment in the. appellant Hospital. Respondent no. 1 filed a claim petition. Initially the claim was filed for Rs.77,07,45,000/- and later the same was amended by claiming a further sum of Rs.20,00,00,000/-. After the case of Malay Kumar Ganguly was remanded by Supreme Court, the National Consumer Disputes Redressal Commission awarded the compensation holding the hospital and the four doctors guilty of medical negligence. The four doctors who had treated the deceased were directed to pay Rs.25,00,000/ - each besides the cost of litigation. The National Commission deducted 10% of the compensation towards the contributory negligence of the claimant holding that he had interfered with the treatment, and awarded G Rs.1,55,58,750/- as compensation payable to the claimant. One of the doctors died· subsequently. The decision of the National Commission was challenged in the instant appeals by the Hospital, the doctors as also by the claimant.

The rival submissions of the parties were but before this Court and the following issues were to be considered by the Court:

1) Whether the claim of the claimant for 8 enhancement of compensation in his appeal is justified. If it is so, for what compensation he is entitled to?

2) While making additional claim by way of affidavit before the National Commission when amending the claim petition, whether the claimant is

entitled for compensation on the enhanced claim preferred before the National Commission?

3(a) Whether the claimant seeking to amend the claim of compensation under certain heads in the original claim petition has forfeited his right of claim under Order II Rule 2 of CPC as pleaded by the Hospital?

3(b) Whether the claimant is justified in claiming additional amount for compensation under different

heads without following the procedure contemplated under the provisions of the Consumer Protection Act and the Rules?

4) Whether the National Commission is justified in adopting the multiplier method to determine the

compensation and to award the compensation in favour of the claimant?

5) Whether the claimant is entitled to pecuniary damages under the heads of loss of employment, loss of his property and his traveling expenses from U.S.A. to India to conduct the proceedings in his claim petition?

6) Whether the claimant is entitled to the interest on the compensation that would be awarded?

7) Whether the compensation awarded in the impugned judgment and the apportionment of the compensation amount fastened upon the doctors and the hospital requires interference and whether the claimant is liable for contributory negligence and deduction of compensation under this head?

8) To what Order and Award the claimant is entitled to in these appeals?

• • •

CHAPTER XXXI

LALITA KUMARI Vs. GOVT. OF U.P. AND ORS. NOVEMBER 12, 2013

Citations: [2013] 14 SCR 713, (2014) 2 SCC 1

[P. SATHASIVAM, CJI., DR. B.S. CHAUHAN, RANJANA PRAKASH DESAI, RANJAN GOGOI AND

S.A. BOBDE, JJ.]

Code of Criminal Procedure, 1973:

s. 154 - FIR - Registration of - Whether mandatory - Or requires the police to conduct preliminary inquiry to test the veracity of such information before registering it - Held: The condition sine qua non for. Registering FIR is that there 0 must be information and the information discloses commission of cognizable offence - The reasonableness or credibility of information is not a condition precedent for the registration of FIR - The provision u/s. 154 is mandatory and therefore it is mandatory for the police officer to register FIR on the basis of information disclosing cognizable offence -

Registration of the FIR is not in contravention of Art. 21 of the Constitution - However, there may be instances where preliminary inquiry may be necessary before registration of FIR e.g. matrimonial disputes, commercial offences, medical negligence cases, corruption cases etc. - However, such inquiry would be only to ascertain as to whether the information reveals any cognizable offence - Constitution of India, 1950 - Article 21. ss.39 and 154(1) - Mandate u/s. 39 to inform about commission of an offence - Implication of - Held: It would be incongruous to suggest that u/s. 39 it is duty of every citizen to inform about commission of an offence, but it is not obligatory for the Officer incharge of the Police Station to register the report uls. 154.

s. 154, 4(2) and 5 - Registration of FIR - Rules in CBI Crime Manual, regarding preliminary inquiry – Applicability 8 of - To s. 154 - The concept of holding preliminary inquiry provided in CBI Crime Manual cannot be imported into the scheme of Cr. P. C. - CBI Crime Manual is not a statute, enacted by legislature but only a set of administrative orders and hence cannot supersede Cr.P.C. - Delhi Special Police Establishment Act, 1946.

Penal Code, 1860- s.166A (as inserted by Criminal Law (Amendment) Act, 2013) - Punishment for non-registration of FIR for the offences specified in the provision – Implication of - Held: The provision under s. 166A does not imply that the registration of FIR is not compulsory for the offences other than those specified in s. 166A - Code of Criminal Procedure, 1973 - s.154.

Constitution of India, 1950:

Art.254(1), Seventh Schedule, Concurrent List Entry 2 and State List Entry 2 - Inconsistency between Laws enacted under Concurrent List and State List - Held: In case of inconsistency, law enacted under Concurrent List will prevail over the law enacted under State List - Hence, provisions of Code of Criminal Procedure (enacted under Entry 2 of Concurrent List) would prevail over the provisions of Police Act and the provisions of Police Act (enacted under State List) would be void to the extent of repugnancy- Therefore, in case of inconsistency between s. 154 Cr.P.C. and s. 44 of Police Act, s. 154 will prevail and s.44 (or similar provisions) shall be void to the extent of repugnancy - Police Act, 1861 - s.44.

Art.21 - Right to life - Whether Violated, if FIR is registered without holding preliminary inquiry - Held: Registration of FIR uls. 154 Cr. P. C. is the 'procedure. established by law' and thus is in conformity with Art.21 - A

Hence registration of FIR as per the provisions of law, does not violate rights guaranteed under Art. 21.

Investigation - Initiation of - By Police - Held: Police is not liable to launch investigation in every FIR which is mandatorily registered uls. 154 Cr.P.C. - Code of Criminal Procedure, 1973 - ss.154 and 157. Police - Police records - FIR Books and General Diary! Daily Diary/Station Diary - Distinction between - Discussed. Interpretation of Statutes - Rule of interpretation – Literal rule of interpretation - Application of - For interpretation of s. 154 Cr.P.C.

Maxim - 'unius est exclusion alterius' - Applicability of - For interpretation of s. 154 Cr.P.C. Words and Phrases - Inquiry - Meaning of, in the context of s. 2(g) of Code of Criminal Procedure, 1973.

The instant cases were referred to Constitution Bench for deciding the question whether a police officer is bound to register a First Information Report (FIR) upon receiving information relating to commission of a cognizable offence u/s. 154 Cr.P.C., or the police officer, has the power to conduct a 'preliminary inquiry' in order to test the veracity of such information before registering the same.

• • •

CHAPTER XXXII

NATIONAL LEGAL SERVICES AUTHORITY Vs. UNION OF INDIA AND OTHERS. APRIL 15, 2014

Citations: [2014] 5 SCR 119, (2014) 5 SCC 438

[K.S. RADHAKRISHNAN AND A.K. SIKRI, JJ.]

CONSTITUTION OF INDIA, 1950:

Article 14 - Transgenders - Claim for equal treatment - Held: Article 14 states that the State shall not deny to "any person" equality before law or equal protection of laws within the territory of India - Article 14 does not restrict the word 'person' and its application only to male or female - Hijras/ transgender persons who are neither male nor female fall o within the expressions 'person' and hence entitle to legal protection of laws in all spheres of state activity including employment, healthcare, education as well as equal civil and citizenship rights as enjoyed by any other Indian citizen - Criminal Tribes Act, 1871 - Penal Code, 1860 - s.377.

Article 14 - Claim by Transgenders/ Hijras launch for legal status as third gender - Held: Transgenders belong to a distinct socio-religious and cultural group and, therefore, have to be considered as a 'third gender' apart from male and female - Gender identity is integral to the dignity of an individual and is at the core of 'personal autonomy' and 'self-determination' - Hijras/ eunuchs, therefore, have to be considered as third gender over and above binary genders -

Article 14, 15, 16, 19 and 21 do no exclude Hijras/TGs from their ambit. Articles 14, 15, 16, 19, 21 - Transgenders - Held: Article 14 use expression "person" and the Article 15 use expression "citizen" and "sex" so also Article 16 - Article 19 a/so use the expression "citizen" - Article 21 use the expression "person" - All these expressions, which are "gender neutral" evidently refer to human-beings - Hence, they take within their sweep Hijras/Transgenders and are not as such limited to male or female gender.

Articles 15 and 16 - Prohibition of discrimination against any citizen on the ground of 'sex' - Held: Both the Articles prohibit all forms of gender bias and gender based discrimination - Expression 'sex' used in Articles 15 and 16 is not just limited to biological sex of male or female but intended to include people who consider themselves to be neither male or female - Bias

- Gender bias.

Article 19(1)(a) - Freedom of speech and expression as to self-identified gender - Held: Freedom of expression includes freedom to express one's chosen gender identity through varied ways and means by way of expression, speech, mannerism, clothing etc. - Transgender's personality could be expressed by Transgender's behavior and presentation - State cannot prohibit, restrict or interfere with

Transgender's expression of such personality which reflects that inherent personality - The values of privacy, self-identity, autonomy and personal integrity are fundamental rights guaranteed to members of the transgender community u/ Article 19(1)(a) and the, State is bound to protect and recognize those rights.

Article 21 - Right to dignity - Transgenders - Held: Article 21 protects the dignity of human life, one's personal autonomy, one's right to privacy - Right to dignity has been recognized to be an essential part of the right to life and accrues to all persons on account of being humans – Right to dignity forms an essential part of our constitutional culture which seeks to ensure the full development and evolution of persons and includes "expressing oneself in diverse forms, freely moving about and mixing with fellow human beings" -

Recognition of one's gender identity lies at the heart of the fundamental right to dignity - Gender constitutes the core of one's sense of being as well as an integral part of a person's identity - Article 21 guarantees the protection of "personal autonomy" of an individual - Self-determination of gender is an integral part of personal autonomy and self-expression and falls within the realm of personal liberty guaranteed under Article 21 of the Constitution of India - Human rights. TRANSGENDERS:

Historical background of Transgenders in India - Discussed.

Gender Identity and sexual orientation - Meaning of -

Held: Gender Identity refers to individual's self-identification as a man, woman or other identified categories – Sexual orientation refers to individual's enduring physical, romantic o and/or emotional attraction to another person.

Rights of transsexual person who have undergone Sex Re-assignment Surgery (SRS) - Test to be applied - Held:

Test to be applied is not the 'Biological test' but 'Psychological test' - U11iversal Declaration of Human Rights, 1948 - Article 6 - International Covenant on Civil and Political Rights, 196.6- Articles 16, 17 - Doctrines/

Principles – Yogyakarta Principles - Human Rights. Problems suffered and discrimination faced by Transgenders - Discussed. Legislations in other countries on Transgenders - Discussed.

Sex identity gender of persons and guarantee to equality and non-discrimination of gender identity - Applicability of, in India - Held: There is no suitable legislation protecting the rights of the members of TG Community - They are facing discrimination in various areas and, therefore, there is necessity to follow the International Conventions to which India is a Party. Gender identity - Whether a person who is born as a male with predominantly female orientation (or vice-versa) has a right to get himself to be recognized as a female as per his 8 choice more so, when such a person after having undergone operational procedure, charges his/her sex as well - Held: If a person has changed his/her sex in tune with his/her gender characteristics and perception which has become possible because of the advancement in medical science and when that is permitted in medical ethics with no legal embargo, there is no impediment, legal or otherwise in giving due recognition to the gender identity based on reassign sex after undergoing SRS.

Sex Re-Assignment Surgery - Legality of - Held: If a person has changed his/her sex in tune with his/her gender characteristics and perception which has become possible because of the advancement in medical science, and when that is permitted by in medical ethics with no legal embargo, there is no impediment, legal or otherwise, in giving due recognition to the gender identity based on the reassign sex after undergoing Sex Re-Assignment Surgery (SRS) - Ethics- Medical ethics.

DOCTRINES/PRINCIPLES: Principle of maximum of happiness to most of the people - Applicability of when claim by transgender for equal status - Held: In such case, there is no dichotomy between the individual freedom/ liberty as against public good - On the contrary, granting the right to choose gender leads to public good.

HUMAN RIGHTS: Held: There is universal recognition that Human rights are rights that "belong" to every person, and do not depend on the specifics of the individual or the relationship between the right-holder and the right-grantor -

Moreover, Human Rights exist irrespective of the question whether they are granted or recognized by the legal and social. system within which we live - They are devices to evaluate A these existing arrangements: ideally, these arrangements should not violate human rights - In other words, human rights are moral, pre-legal rights - They are not granted by people nor can they be taken away by them.

INTERNATIONAL CONVENTION: Implementation of -

Held: Implementation of International Convention requires legislation - Article 253 states that Parliament has power to make any law for the whole or any part of territory of India for implementing any treaty, agreement or convention - Indian courts can apply rules of international law according to the principles of Comity of nations, unless they are overridden by clear rules of domestic law - Constitution· of India, 1950 - Articles 51, 253.

INTERNATIONAL LAW: Binding effect of - Held: If Parliament has made any legislation which is in conflict with the International law, then Indian courts are bound to give effect to the Indian Law rather than international law -

Constitution of India, 1950 - Articles 51, 253.

JURISPRUDENCE: Theory of law - Kantian criterion of justice - Interpretation of - Discussed.

_ WORDS AND PHRASES: Transgender - Held: It is generally described as an umbrella term for persons whose gender identity, gender expression or behavior does not conform to their biological sex - Transgender may also takes in persons who do not identify with their sex assigned at birth, which include Hijras/Eunuchs - TG Community comprises of Hijras, eunuchs, Kothis, Aravanis, Jogappas, Shiv-Shakthis etc. - Etymologically, the term 'transgender' is derived from two words, namely 'trans' and 'gender' - Former is a Latin word which means 'across' or 'beyond' - The grammatical meaning of 'transgender', therefore, is across or beyond gender – This has come to be known as umbrella term which includes Gay men, Lesbians, bisexuals, and cross dressers within its scope Transgenderism is not a disease at all but a benign normal variant of human experience akin to left handedness.

The instant writ petitions were filed by the members of Transgender Community for declaration of their gender identity than the one assigned to them, male or female, at the time of birth. Their prayer is that non-recognition of their gender identity violates Articles 14 and 21 of the Constitution of India. Hijras/Eunuchs, who also fall in that group, also claimed legal status as a third gender with all legal and constitutional protection.

The questions for consideration in these writ petitions were whether a person who is born as a male with predominantly female orientation (or vice-versa), has a right to get himself to be recognized as a female (or vice-versa) as per his/her choice more so, when such a person after having undergone operational procedure, changes his/her sex as well; whether transgender (TG), who are neither males nor females, have a right to be identified and categorized as a "third gender".

• • •

CHAPTER XXXIII

PRAMATI EDUCATIONAL & CULTURAL TRUST & ORS. Vs. UNION OF INDIA & ORS. MAY 06, 2014

Citations: [2014] 11 SCR 712, (2014) 8 SCC 1

[R.M. LODHA, CJI, A.K. PATNAIK, SUDHANSU JYOTI MUKHOPADHAYA DIPAK MISRA AND FAKKIR MOHAMED IBRAHIM KALIFULLA, JJ.]

Constitution of India, 1950:

Art. 15(5) [as inserted by Constitution (Ninety-Third Amendment) Act, 2005] and Arts. 14, 19(1)(g) and 21 - Constitutional validity of Art. 15(5) - Held: Art. 15(5) does not alter the basic structure and framework of the Constitution - The provision is also not violative of the concept of secularism - None of the rights under Articles 14, 19(1)(g) and 21 have been abrogated by clause (5) of Article 15 and hence, it is constitutionally valid.

Article 21 A [as inserted by Constitution (Eighty-Sixty Amendment) Act, 2002] 19(1)(g) and 30(1) – Constitutional validity of Art. 21A -There is nothing in Art. 21A which conflicts with either the right of private unaided schools under Article 19(1)(g) or the right of minority schools under Article 30(1) -

However, the law made under Art. 21A if abrogates the rights under Articles 19(1)(g) and 30(1), can be held ultra vires the Constitution - Right of Children to Free and Compulsory Education Act, which was enacted under Article 21A, in so far as it was made applicable to aided minority schools is ultra vires the Constitution - Right of Children to Free and Compulsory Education Act, 2009.

• • •

CHAPTER XXXIV

M/S. KAILASH NATH ASSOCIATES Vs. DELHI DEVELOPMENT AUTHORITY & ANR. JANUARY 09, 2015

Citations: [2015] 1 SCR 627, (2015) 4 SCC 136

[RANJAN GOGOI AND R.F. NARIMAN, JJ.]

Contract Act, 1872 - Public auction - Earnest money - Forfeiture of - Appellant, highest bidder for plot deposited 25% of the bid amount-earnest money (Rs 78 lakhs) with ODA - Balance 75% was to be deposited within three months - Extension of time for payment by DOA twice - Thereafter, several letters written by the appellant to DOA but no response - Subsequently, letter written by ODA to the appellant that his case was referred to UOI for its approval for condoning the delay, case being one of Nazul land, which was later declared by the Central Government as non-Nazul land - On DDA's request, appellant consented to making payment of the balance amount with interest charged - After few years cancellation of allotment of the plot by ODA and consequent forfeiture of the earnest money - Suit for specific performance and damages and recovery of earnest amount by the' appellant - Subsequently DOA re-auctioned the premises fetching Rs. 11. 78 crores - Dismissal of suit by the Single Judge of the High Court but ordered refund of the earnest money forfeited with 9% interest p.a. - However, Division

Bench upheld forfeiture of the earnest money - On appeal, held: It was arbitrary for the DOA to forfeit the earnest money - In the absence of notice to deposit the balance 75% amount within a certain stated time, there is no breach of contract on the part of the appellant and consequently earnest money could not be forfeited - ODA not having been put to any loss, even if ODA could insist on a contractual stipulation in its favour, it would be arbitrary to allow DOA as a public authority to appropriate Rs. 78 lakhs without any loss being caused - Article 14 would apply - In fact, DOA made huge profit on reauction of the plot - If damage or loss is not suffered, the law does not provide for a windfall - Thus, the judgment of the Single Judge of the High Court restored - Constitution of India, 1950 - Article 14. s. 7 4 - Compensation for breach of contract where penalty stipulated for under -

General principles - Enunciated.

• • •

CHAPTER XXXV

SHREYA SINGHAL Vs. UNION OF INDIA. MARCH 24, 2015

Citations: [2015] 5 SCR 963, (2015) 5 SCC 01

[J. CHELAMESWAR AND R. F. NARIMAN, JJ.]

Information Technology Act, 2000:

s. 66A - Constitutional validity of - Held: s. 66A is violative of Article 19(1)(a) and is not saved under Article 19(2) – It arbitrarily, excessively and disproportionately invades the right of free speech and upsets the balance between such rights and the reasonable restrictions imposed thereupon - the expressions used in s. 66A are open ended, vague and undefined - The reach of the section is such that it has a chilling effect on free speech and thus suffers from the vice of overbreadth - Therefore, s. 66A as a whole is declared unconstitutional - Constitution of India, 1950 -Art. 19(1) (a) and 19(2).

s. 66A - Whether constitutionally invalid on the touchstone of Art. 14 of the Constitution - Held: There is an intelligible differentia between speech on the internet and other mediums of communication - Hence s. 66A is not violative of Art. 14 - Constitution of India, 1950-Art. 14.

s. 69A and Information Technology (Procedure and Safeguards for Blocking for Access of Information by Public) G Rules, 2009 - Constitutional validity of- Held: s. 69A as well as the Rules are constitutionally valid - s. 69A is a narrowly drawn provision with several safeguards under the Rules -

Merely absence of certain additional safeguards as provided u/ss. 95 and 96 Cr. P. C. does not make the Rules constitutionally infirm - Information Technology (Procedure and Safeguards for Blocking for Access of Information by Public) Rules, 2009- Code of Criminal Procedure, 1973- ss. 95 and 96.

B s. 79 and Information Technology (Intermediary Guidelines) Rules, 2011- Constitutional validity of- Held: s. 79 is valid, subject to s. 79(3)(b) being read down to mean that an intermediary upon receiving actual knowledge from a court order or on being modified by the appropriate Government or its agency that unlawful acts relatable to article 19(2) are going to be committed, and then fails to expeditiously remove or disable access to such material - Similarly the Rules are valid, subject tor. 3(4) being read down in the same manner as s. 79(3)(b) - Information Technology (Intermediary Guidelines) Rules, 2011- r. 3(4).

Kerala Police Act, 1960: s. 118 - Legislative competence of- Challenged - Held:

The Act as a whole ands. 118 as part thereof falls in pith and substance within Entry 2 List II of Seventh Schedule of the Constitution - Even otherwise, the penalty created for causing annoyance in an indecent manner in pith and substance would fall within Entry 1 List Ill and would thus be within the competence of the State Legislature – Constitution of India, 1950- Seventh schedule, List II, Entry 2; List Ill Entry

1 - Doctrine of Pith and Substance.

s. 118 - Constitutional validity of - Held: s. 118 suffers from the vice of vagueness and overbreadth - Thus violates Art. 19(1)(a) and since not saved under any of the subject matters contained in Art. 19(2), hence is unconstitutional.

Statutes - Challenge to the vires of - Ground for - Held:

Possibility of abuse of a statute is not a ground to test its validity, if the statute is otherwise valid.

Doctrine of Severability -Applicability of- Discussed.

Words and Phrases:

'Reasonable restrictions' - Meaning of, in the context of Art. 19(2) of the Constitution.

HELD: When it comes to democracy, liberty of thought and expression is a cardinal value that is of

paramount significance under the constitutional scheme. There are three concepts which are fundamental in understanding the reach of this most basic of human rights i.e. "freedom of speech and expression". The first is discussion, the second is advocacy, and the third is incitement. Mere discussion or even advocacy of a particular cause howsoever unpopular it is at the heart of Article 19(1)(a). It is only when such discussion or advocacy reaches the level of incitement that Article 19(2) kicks in~ It is at this stage that a law may be made curtailing the speech or · expression that leads inexorably to or tends to cause public disorder or tends to cause or tends to affect the sovereignty & integrity of India, the security of the State, friendly relations with foreign States, etc. (Paras 8 and 13] [987-F; 991-A-C]

• • •

CHAPTER XXXVI

SUPREME COURT ADVOCATES-ON-RECORD ASSOCIATION AND ANOTHER Vs. UNION OF INDIA . OCTOBER 16, 2015

Citations: [2015] 13 SCR 1, 2016 (5) SCC 1

[JAGDISH SINGH KHEHAR, J. CHELAMESWAR, MADAN B. LOKUR, KURIAN JOSEPH, ADARSH KUMAR GOEL, JJ.]

Constitution (Ninety-ninth Amendment) Act, 2014 - Collegium system of appointment of Judges to the Supreme Court, and Chief Justices and Judges to the High Courts; and transfer of Chief Justices and Judges of High Courts from one High Court, to another- New scheme contemplated for replacing the Collegium system - Six-member National Judicial Appointments Commission (NJAC) set up under the aegis of Constitution (Ninety-ninth Amendment) Act, 2014 read with the National Judicial Appointments Commission Act, 2014-NJAC composed of: (a) the Chief Justice of India, Chairperson, ex officio; ·(b) two other senior Judges of Supreme Court, next to the Chief Justice of India as Members, ex officio; (c) the Union Minister in charge of Law and Justice as Member, ex officio; (d) two eminent persons, to be nominated as Members - Constitution (Ninety-ninth Amendment) Act, 2014 - Validity of- Held (per order of the Court): It is unconstitutional and void - National Judicial Appointments Commission Act, 2014 - Judiciary- Higher Judiciary- Constitutional Courts -Appointment and transfer

of Judges - Procedure.

National Judicial Appointments Commission Act, 2014

- Collegium system of appointment of Judges to the Supreme Court, and Chief Justices and Judges to the High Courts; and transfer of Chief Justices and Judges of High Courts from one High Court, to another- New scheme contemplated for replacing the Collegium system - Six-member National Judicial Appointments Commission (NJAC) set up under the aegis of Constitution (Ninety-ninth Amendment) Act, 2014 read with the National Judicial Appointments Commission Act, 2014- NJAC composed of: (a) the Chief Justice of India, Chairperson, ex officio; (b} two other senior Judges of Supreme Court, next to the Chief Justice of India as Members, ex officio; (c) the Union Minister in charge of Law and Justice as Member, ex officio; (d} two eminent persons, to be nominated as Members - National Judicial Appointments Commission Act, 2014 - Validity of – Held (per order of the Court): It is unconstitutional and void - Constitution (Ninety-ninth Amendment) Act, 2014- Judiciary - Higher Judiciary - Constitutional Courts – Appointment and transfer of Judges- Procedure. Judiciary - Higher Judiciary- Constitutional Courts - Appointment and transfer of Judges-Procedure- Collegium system of appointment of Judges to the Supreme Court, and Chief Justices and Judges to the High Courts; and transfer of Chief Justices and Judges of High Courts from one High Court, to another- New scheme contemplated for replacing the Collegium system - Six-member National Judicial Appointments Commission (NJAC) set up under the aegis of Constitution (Ninety-ninth Amendment) Act, 2014 read with the National Judicial Appointments Commission Act, 2014 - NJAC composed of: (a) the Chief Justice of India, Chairperson, ex officio; (b) two other senior Judges of Supreme Court, next to the Chief Justice of India as Members, ex officio; (c) the Union Minister in charge of Law and Justice as Member, ex officio; (d) two eminent persons, to be nominated as Members- Held (per order of the Court):

The collegium system, as existing prior to the Constitution (Ninety-ninth Amendment) Act, 2014, declared to be operative - However, to consider introduction of appropriate measures, if any, for an improved working of the "collegium system", matter listed on a subsequent date.:. Constitution (Ninety-ninth Amendment) Act, 2014 - National Judicial Appointments Commission Act, 2014. Judiciary ~ Higher judiciary - Constitutional Courts - Selection and appointment of Judges - Parliament, if

empowered to provide for an alternative procedure – Held (per Khehar, J.): It is open to the Parliament, while exercising its power under Article 368, to provide for some other alternative procedure for the selection and appointment of Judges to the higher judiciary, so long as, the attributes of "separation of powers" and "independence of the judiciary", which are "core" components of the "basic structure" of the Constitution, are maintained.

Constitution of India -Amendment to - Scope – Held (per Khehar, J.): The "basic structure" of the Constitution is inviolable ~ The Constitution cannot be amended so as to negate any "basic features" thereof-Also, if a challenge is raised to an ordinary legislation based on one of the "basic features" of the Constitution, it would be valid to do so. Constitution of

India - Art. 368 – Constitutional Amendments - Will of the People and Judicial Review - Limitations on the amending power - Appointment and transfer of Judges in higher judiciary- Broad based Judicial Appointment Commission comprising of members of the judiciary, the executive and eminent! important persons from public life 'proposed to be constituted, to replace the prevailing procedure, contemplated under Articles 124(2) and 217(1)- To achieve the purported objective, Articles 124 and 217 inter alia amended, and Articles 124A, 1248 and 124C inserted in the Constitution, through the Constitution (99th Amendment) Act, by following the procedure contemplated.

• • •

CHAPTER XXXVII

UNION OF INDIA Vs. SRI HARAN@ MURUGAN & ORS. DECEMBER 02, 2015

Citations: [2015] 14 SCR 613, 2016 (7) SCC 1

[H. L. DATTU, CJI, FAKKIR MOHAMED IBRAHIM KALIFULLA, PINAKI CHANDRA GHOSE,ABHAY MANOHAR SAPRE AND UDAY UMESH LAUT, JJ.)

Criminal - Remission of sentence - Present petition filed for quashing of letter issued by Government of Tamil Nadu wherein State of Tamil Nadu proposes to remit sentence of life imprisonment and to release Respondents who were convicted in Rajiv Gandhi Assassination case in pursuance of commutation of death sentence - Whether exercise of power of remission under Section 432 of Code by State of Tamil Nadu in case of Respondents was impermissible - Held, Petitioner relied on Swamy Shraddananda v. State of Karnataka to state that life imprisonment imposed on commutation of death penalty will mean till end of life and, thus, beyond exercise of power of remission - Therefore, Petitioner contended that exercise of power of remission under Section 432 of Code by State of Tamil Nadu in case of Respondents was impermissible - It was not appropriate for three Judges' Bench to examine and decide correctness of verdict of another three-Judges' Bench in Swamy Shraddananda (supra) - Considering wider interpretation of provisions of Constitution and Code involved in matter, consider it fit to refer matter to Constitution Bench for authoritative interpretation on same - Matter referred to constitution bench - Petition disposed of. [paras 40, 41, 42 and 46].

This writ petition, Under Article 32 of the Constitution of India, has been filed by the Union of India praying for quashing of letter dated 19.02.2014, issued by the Chief Secretary, Government of Tamil Nadu to the Secretary, Government of India wherein the State of Tamil Nadu proposes to remit the sentence of life imprisonment and to release Respondent Nos. 1-7 herein who were convicted in the Rajiv Gandhi Assassination Case in pursuance of commutation of death sentence of Respondent Nos. 1-3 herein by this Court on 18.02.2014 in this case.

Pursuant to the judgment of this Court dated 18.02.2014 in v. Sriharan @ Murugan (supra), the Government of Tamil Nadu took a decision to grant remission to Respondent Nos. 1 to 7. Accordingly, the Government of Tamil Nadu sent a letter dated 19.02.2014 to the Secretary to the Government of India, Ministry of Home Affairs, stating that it proposes to remit the sentence of life imprisonment. It was asserted in the letter that since the crime was investigated by the Central Bureau of Investigation (CBI) and as per Section 435 of the Code of Criminal Procedure, 1973 (in short "the Code"), the State Government, while exercising its power Under Section 432 of the Code, must act after consultation with the Central Government, accordingly, it requested to indicate the views of the Union of India within three days on the proposal to release the seven persons.

Accordingly, in these matters, we are called upon to decide the legitimacy of the proposal of the State Government to release Respondent Nos. 1 to 7, who are facing life sentence. For the purpose of disposal of the issue in question, we reiterate the relevant provisions. Sections 432 and 435 of the Code.

• • •

CHAPTER XXXVIII

GUJARAT URJA VIKAS NIGAM LIMITED Vs. EMCO LIMITED & OTHERS. FEBRUARY 02, 2016

Citations: [2016] 1 SCR 857, (2016) 11 SCC 182

[J. CHELAMESWAR AND ABHAY MANOHAR SAPRE, JJ.]

Electricity - Tariff determination - For procurement of power by Distribution Licensees in Gujarat from Solar Energy Projects - Tariff determination by order dated 29.1.2010 (first tariff order) taking into account the benefit of accelerated depreciation under s.32 of the Income Tax Act and Rules - The order also. Provided for determination of separate tariff for the project which did not get the benefit of accelerated depreciation - Appellant entered into Power Purchase Agreement (PPA) for sale and purchase of electricity with the respondent-power producer for the project to be established by it - However, could not commence generation of power within control period stipulated under first tariff order - Another order dated 27.1.2012 (second tariff order) determining the tariff applicable to the projects to be commissioned on or after 29.1.2012 - The power producer commenced generation of power subsequent to second tariff order - The power producers petition to State Commission for permission to. claim tariff as per second tariff order, allowed - Order of State Commission confirmed by the Appellate Tribunal - On appeal, held: The terms of the PPA does not entitle the power producer to the tariff as determined by the Second tariff order - 'The benefit of accelerated promotion 'flows from the Income Tax Act which was dependent on the option of the power producer - PPA does not make any reference to such benefit - The availability of the option does not relieve the power producer of the contractual obligations incurred under the PPA – Therefore the power producer is not entitled to tariff as per second tariff order.

• • •

CHAPTER XXXIX

MUKESH & ANR. Vs. STATE FOR NCT OF DELHI & ORS. MAY,2017

Citations: [2017] 6 SCR 1, (2017) 6 SCC 1

[DIPAK MISRA, R. BANUMATHI AND ASHOK BHUSHAN, JJ.]

Criminal - Capital punishment - Gang rape - Rarest of rare category - Sections 120B, 201, 302, 307, 365, 366, 376(2)(g), 377, 395, 397 and 412 of Indian Penal Code, 1860 and Sections 235 and 354 of Code of Criminal Procedure, 1973 - Deceased prosecutrix and informant boarded bus - Accused persons started to abuse informant and assaulted him with iron rods - Robbed their articles - Prosecutrix was raped by them, one after other - Prosecutrix was also subjected to unnatural sex - Her private parts and her internal organs were seriously injured - Accused were exhorting that both victims be not left alive - Threw them out of moving bus - Victims were taken to Hospital - First Information Report was registered - 1st Accused was arrested - Personal search was conducted and his disclosure statement - Investigating Officer seized bus - Arrest of 1st Accused, led to arrest of 4th and 5th Accused - Later on, 2nd Accused was apprehended - Mobile belonging to informant was recovered - In Test Identification Parade, informant identified 2nd Accused - Further recoveries were made - Dying declaration of prosecutrix was recorded - Prosecutrix gave her statement through gestures and writings - Later on, in foreign hospital, prosecutrix died - Charge-sheet came to be filed under provisions of Code, 1860 - Supplementary charge sheet was filed later on - During course of trial, 1st Accused committed suicide - Sessions Judge convicted all Accused persons under Sections 120B, 365, 366, 307, 376(2)(g), 377, 302, 395, 397, 201 and 412 - All Accused were sentenced to death for offence - Punishment of imprisonment was also awarded - Fine was also imposed - High Court affirmed conviction and confirmed death penalty - Hence, present appeals by all Accused/Appellants - Whether Accused persons were guilty of their culpability or there was public pressure, as alleged, to falsely implicate them - Whether Courts below did not follow fundamental norms of sentencing and were not guided by paramount beacons of legislative policy discernible from Sections 354(3) and 235(2) of Code, 1973 - Whether there was violation of mandate of Section 235(2) of Code,

1973 - Whether present case could be one of rarest of rare cases warranting death penalty.

Held while dismissing the appeal,

The law laid down above, clearly sets forth the sentencing policy evolved over a period of time. I now proceed to analyse the facts and circumstances of the present case on the anvil of above-stated principles. To be very precise, the nature and the manner of the act committed by the accused, and the effect it casted on the society and on the victim's family, are to be weighed against the mitigating circumstances stated by the accused and the scope of their reform, so as to reach a definite reasoned conclusion as to what would be appropriate punishment in the present case- 'death sentence', life sentence commutable to 14 years' or 'life imprisonment for the rest of the life'.

The question would be whether the present case could be one of the rarest of rare cases warranting death penalty. Before the court proceed to make a choice whether to award death sentence or life imprisonment, the court is to draw up a balance-sheet of aggravating and mitigating circumstances attending to the commission of the offence and then strike a balance between those aggravating and mitigating circumstances. Two questions are to be asked and answered: (i) Is there something uncommon about the crimes which regard sentence of imprisonment for life inadequate; (ii) Whether there is no alternative punishment suitable except death sentence. Where a crime is committed with extreme brutality and the collective conscience of the society is shocked, courts must award death penalty, irrespective of their personal opinion as regards desirability of death penalty. By not imposing a death sentence in such cases, the courts may do injustice to the society at large.

We are here concerned with the award of an appropriate sentence case of brutal gang-rape and murder of a young lady, involving most gruesome and barbaric act of inserting iron rods in the private parts of the victim. The act was committed in connivance and collusion of six who were on a notorious spree running a bus, showcasing as a public transport, with the intent of attracting passengers and committing crime with them. The victim and her friend were picked up from the Munirka bus stand with the mala fide intent of ravishing and torturing her. The accused not only abducted the victim, but gang-raped her, committed unnatural offence by compelling her for oral sex, bit her lips, cheeks, breast and caused horrifying injuries to her private parts by inserting iron rod which ruptured the vaginal rectum, jejunum and rectum. The diabolical manner in which crime was committed leaves one startled as to the pervert mental state of the inflictor. On top of it, after having failed to kill her on the spot, by running the bus over her, the victim was thrown half naked in the wintery night, with grievous injuries.

If we look at the aggravating circumstances in the present case, following factors would emerge:

• Diabolic nature of the crime and the manner of committing crime, as reflected in committing gang-rape with the victim; forcing her to perform oral sex, injuries on the body of the deceased by way of bite marks; insertion of iron rod in her private parts and causing fatal injuries to her private parts and other internal injuries; pulling out her internal organs which caused sepsis and ultimately led to her death; throwing the victim and the complainant (P.W. 1) naked in the cold wintery night and trying to run the bus over them.

• The brazenness and coldness with which the acts were committed in the evening hours by picking up the deceased and the victim from a public space, reflects the threat to which the society would be posed to, in case the accused are not appropriately punished. More so, it reflects that there is no scope of reform.

• The horrific acts reflecting the in-human extent to which the accused could go to satisfy their lust, being completely oblivious, not only to the norms of the society, but also to the norms of humanity.

• The acts committed so shook the conscience of the society.

As noted earlier, on the aspect of sentencing, seeking reduction of death sentence to life imprisonment, three of the convicts/Appellants namely A-3 Akshay, A-4 Vinay and A-5 Pawan placed on record, through their individual affidavits dated 23.03.2017, following mitigating circumstances:

(a) Family circumstances such as poverty and rural background,

(b) Young age,

(c) Current family situation including age of parents, ill health of family members and their responsibilities towards their parents and other family members,

(d) Absence of criminal antecedents,

(e) Conduct in jail, and

(f) Likelihood of reformation.

In his affidavit, accused Mukesh reiterated his innocence and only pleaded that he is falsely implicated in the case.

In Purushottam Dashrath Borate and Anr. v. State of Maharashtra MANU/SC/0583/2015 (2015) 6 SCC 652, this Court held that age of the accused or family background of the accused or lack of criminal antecedents cannot be said to be the mitigating circumstance. It cannot also be considered as mitigating circumstance, particularly taking into consideration, the nature of heinous offence and cold and calculated manner in which it was committed by the accused persons.

Society's reasonable expectation is that deterrent punishment commensurate with the gravity of the offence be awarded. When the crime is brutal, shocking the collective conscience of the community, sympathy in any form would be misplaced and it would shake the confidence of public in the administration of criminal justice system. As held in Om Prakash v. State of Haryana MANU/SC/0129/1999: (1999) 3 SCC 19, the Court must respond to the cry of the society and to settle what would be a deterrent punishment for what was an apparently abominable crime.

Bearing in mind the above principles governing the sentencing policy, I have considered all the aggravating and mitigating circumstances in the present case. Imposition of appropriate punishment is the manner in which the courts respond to the society's cry for justice against the crime. Justice demands that the courts should impose punishments befitting the crime so that it reflects public abhorrence of the crime. Crimes like the one before us cannot be looked with magnanimity. Factors like young age of the accused and poor background cannot be said to be mitigating circumstances. Likewise, post-crime remorse and post-crime good conduct of the accused, the statement of the accused as to their background and family circumstances, age, absence of criminal antecedents and their good conduct in prison, in my view, cannot be taken as mitigating circumstances to take the case out of the category of "rarest of rare cases". The circumstances stated by the accused in their affidavits are too slender to be treated as mitigating circumstances.

In the present case, there is not even a hint of hesitation in my mind with respect to the aggravating circumstances outweighing the mitigating circumstances and I do not find any justification to convert the death sentence imposed by the courts below to 'life imprisonment for the rest of the life'. The gruesome offences were committed with highest viciousness. Human lust was allowed to take such a demonic form. The accused may not be hardened criminals; but the cruel manner in which the gang-rape was committed in the moving bus; iron rods were inserted in the private parts of the victim; and the coldness with which both the victims were thrown naked in cold wintery night of December, shocks the collective conscience of the society. The present case clearly comes within the category of 'rarest of rare case' where the question of any other punishment is 'unquestionably foreclosed'. If at all there is a case warranting award of death sentence, it is the present case. If the dreadfulness displayed by the accused in committing the gang-rape, unnatural sex, insertion of iron rod in the private parts of the victim does not fall in the 'rarest of rare category', then one may wonder what else would fall in that category. On these reasoning recorded by me, I concur with the majority in affirming the death sentence awarded to the accused persons.

The incident of gang-rape on the night of 16.12.2012 in the capital sparked public protest not only in Delhi but nation-wide. We live in a civilized society where law and order is supreme and the citizens enjoy inviolable fundamental human rights. But when the incident of gang-rape like the present one surfaces, it causes ripples in the conscience of society and serious doubts are raised as to whether we really live in a civilized society and whether both men and women feel the same sense of liberty and freedom which they should have felt in the ordinary course of a civilized society, driven by rule of law. Certainly, whenever such grave violations of human dignity come to fore, an unknown sense of insecurity and helplessness grabs the entire society, women in particular, and the only succor people look for, is the State to take command of the situation and remedy it effectively.

The statistics of National Crime Records Bureau which I have indicated in the beginning of my judgment show that despite the progress made by women in education and in various fields and changes brought in ideas of women's rights, respect for women is on the decline and crimes against women are on the increase. Offences against women are not a women's issue alone but, human rights issue. Increased rate of crime against women is an area of concern for the law-makers and it points out an emergent need to study in depth the root of the problem and remedy the same through a strict law and order regime. There are a number of legislations and numerous penal provisions to punish the offenders of violence against women. However, it becomes important to ensure that gender justice does not remain only on paper.

We have a responsibility to set good values and guidance for posterity. In the words of great scholar, Swami Vivekananda, "the best thermometer to the progress of a nation is its treatment of its women." Crime against women not only affects women's self-esteem and dignity but also degrades the pace of societal development. I hope that this gruesome incident in the capital and death of this young woman will be an eye-opener for a mass movement "to end violence against women" and "respect for women and her dignity" and sensitizing public at large on gender justice. Every individual, irrespective of his/her gender must be willing to assume the responsibility in fight for gender justice and also awaken public opinion on gender justice. Public at large, in particular men, are to be sensitized on gender justice. The battle for gender justice can be won only with strict implementation of legislative provisions, sensitization of public, taking other pro-active steps at all levels for combating violence against women and ensuring widespread attitudinal changes and comprehensive change in the existing mind set. We hope that this incident will pave the way for the same.

• • •

CHAPTER XL

EXCEL CROP CARE LIMITED Vs. COMPETITION COMMISSION OF INDIA AND ANOTHER. MAY 08, 2017

Citations: [2017] 5 SCR 901, (2017) 8 SCC 47

[A. K. SIKRI AND N. V. RAMANA, JJ.]

Competition Act, 2002:

ss. 3(3)(a), 3(3}(b) and 3(3)(d) rlw. s. 3(1) and ss. 26(1),27(b) - Complaint by Food Corporation of India (FCI) -Alleging that the three appellant companies and one more company had arrived at anti-competitive agreement in relation to tenders issued by FCI for Aluminum Phosphide Tablets (APT) between the years 2007 and 2009 - Competition Commission of India (CCI) directed investigation - Director General (DG) gave report giving prima facie .finding affirming the allegations - CCI concluded that the appellant-companies entered into anti-competitive agreement in concerted manner thereby offending the provisions of s.3 and imposed penalties on all the three appellants at 9% of average 3 years turnover - Competition Appellate Tribunal confirmed the finding of CCI - However, reduced the penalty holding that the penalty at 9% cannot be on the 'total turnover' and has to be restricted to 9% of the 'relevant turnover' - On appeal questions whether s. 3 was applicable in respect of tender issued prior to coming into force of s. 3; whether CCI was barred from investigating the matter pertaining to tender floated in 20 JI as there was no complaint about that tender; whether .finding as regards collusive bidding was justified and whether the penalty has to be on 'total turnover' or only on the 'relevant turnover' of the offending company - Held: Section 3 would be applicable in respect of the tender issued prior to coming into force of s. 3 as well because the anti-competitive conduct of the offending companies continued even after coming into force of s. 3 - 2011 tender also could be the subject-matter of inquiry even when it was not referred to in the complaint - Section 26(1) is wide enough to cover the investigation by DG - While carrying out such investigation, il other facts also

get revealed, DG would be well within its power to include those as well in his report - In the facts of the case. the ingredients of s. 3 stand satisfied and the CCI rightly held that provisions of s. 3(3)(a), 3(3)(b) and 3(3)(d) have been contravened by appellant companies - Section 27(b), while prescribing the penalty on the 'turnover', neither uses the prefix 'total' nor 'relevant' - In the absence of specific provision as to whether such turnover has to be product specific or entire turnover of the offending company, adopting the criteria of 'relevant turnover 'for the purpose of imposition of penalty will be more in tune with ethos ol the Act and the legal principles pertaining to imposition of penalties. Interpretation of Statutes: lnterpretation of penal statute - Per Sikri, J.: Interpretation which brings out inequitable or absurd results has to be eschewed - Even if two interpretation are possible, one that leans in favor of the finger has to be adopted, on the principle of strict interpretation that needs to be given to such statutes – Per Ramana, J.: Where interpretative exercise involves various equitable facets, literal interpretation might not be conclusive – An interpretation should sub-serve the intent and purpose of the statutory provision.

Doctrines/Principles:

Doctrine of proportionality - Applicability of- Discussed.

Doctrine of purposive interpretation - Applicability of:

Principle of 'Noscitur a sociis' - Applicability of. Dismissing the appeals, the Court

HELD: Per A. K. Sikri, J.: 1.1 Though, the Competition Act is of the year 2002 and was passed by the Legislature on 13 January, 2003, as per the provisions of Section 1(3) thereof, the Act was to come into force from the date to be notified by the Central Government in the Official Gazette. Notification was issued by the Central Government wherein 31" March, 2003 was specified as the appointed date. However, vide this notification, some of the provisions of the Act, and not all the provisions, were enforced. Section 3 of the Act came into force on 20 May, 2009 vide S.O. 124l(E) dated 15'h May, 2009 on which date the said notification was published in the Gazette of India as well. [Para 11 I [928-B-D I

• • •

CHAPTER XLI

COMMON CAUSE Vs. UNION OF INDIA AND ORS. AUGUST 2, 2017

Citations: [2017] 13 SCR 361, (2017) 9 SCC 499

[MADAN B. LOKUR AND DEEPAK GUPTA, JJ.]

Mines and Minerals – Illegal mining of enormous proportions in districts of Odisha – Writ petition partly based on reports given by Justice M.B. Shah Commissions of Inquiry sought directions, inter alia, to Union of India and Government of Odisha to immediately stop forthwith all illegal mining in the State of Odisha and for CBI investigation into such illegal mining – Plea of mining lease holders that reports given by Commission were vitiated as they were not given notice u/ss.8B, 8C of the 1952 Act, and thus, the very foundation of the writ petition goes away – Held: First report given by Commission was a general, overall perspective on the subject – No irregularity or illegality has been committed so as to vitiate the first report – Second report went into specific details of several mining lease holders, but herein one is not concerned with those specifics – Therefore, whether notices were issued or not to the lease holders who were the subject matter of discussion in the second report is of no consequence –However, the reports of the Commission are not being relied upon for the purpose of present judgment and order – Further, for now, no direction is being given with regard to any investigation by CBI – Expert Committee be set up under the guidance of a retired judge of Supreme Court to identify the lapses occurred over the years enabling rampant illegal or unlawful mining in Odisha and measures to prevent this from happening in other parts of the country – Further, directions issued – Commissions of Inquiry Act, 1952 – ss.8B, 8C.

Committees:

Central Empowered Committee (CEC) – Constitution of – Held: CEC was first constituted by Supreme Court in T. N. Godavarman case as an interim body – Thereafter, it was constituted by notification issued u/s.3(3) of the 1986 Act – It has continued functioning and is now an established body which renders extremely valuable advice to this Court – Environment (Protection) Act, 1986 – s.3(3).

Central Empowered Committee (CEC) – Jurisdiction of – Challenge to – Plea of lease holders that in giving the report on mining, CEC exceeded its remit – Held: Not tenable – Jurisdiction of CEC was not limited and it was expected to give a detailed report on all aspects of illegal mining or mining being carried out without any lawful authority in whatever manner.

Mines and Minerals (Development and Regulation) Act, 1957 (MMDR) – ss.4(1), 4(2), 5(2), 10, 12, 13, 18, 21 – Grant of mining lease – Scheme of – Discussed. s.6 – Maximum area for which a prospecting license or mining lease may be granted – Violation of, by various companies – If any – Discussed.

Mineral Concession Rules, 1960 (MCR):

Distinction between MCR and MCDR – Held: The distinction is that the MCR deal, inter alia, with the grant of a mining lease and not commencement of mining operations – However, the MCDR deal, inter alia, with the commencement of mining operations and protection of environment by preventing and controlling pollution which might be caused by mining operations– Mineral Conservation and Development Rules, 1988 (MCDR).

r.22A – Held: r.22A makes it clear that mining operations shall be undertaken only in accordance with the duly approved mining plan – Therefore, a mining plan is of considerable importance for a mining lease holder and is in essence sacrosanct – A mining scheme and a mining plan are a sine qua non for the grant of a mining lease.

r.24A – Plea of mining lease holders that since many of them were granted first deemed statutory renewal of mining lease u/r.24A, the requirements of Environment Impact Assessment (EIA) Notification of 1994 (EIA 1994) would not be applicable – Held: Not tenable –

For renewal of mining lease, an application is required to be made by mining lease holders and the deemed renewal clause u/r.24A will come into operation only after an application for renewal is made in Form J in Schedule I of MCR – Even otherwise, renewal of a mining lease would require a prior environmental clearance (EC) in terms of EIA 1994.

r.37 – Violation of – Several mining lease holders entered into raising contracts which were actually a transfer of lease as postulated by r.37 – Held: Rule 37 provides, inter alia, that a mining lessee shall not without the previous consent in writing of the State Government or Central Government, as the case may be, assign, sublet, mortgage, or in any other manner, transfer the mining lease, or any right, title or interest therein – It will be appropriate if a fresh look is given to the raising contracts entered into by mining lease holders and the raising contractor – Committee appointed.

Mineral Conservation and Development Rules, 1988 (MCDR):

Purpose and objective of – Held: Is to ensure that mining operations are carried out in a scientific manner with a high degree of responsibility including responsibility in protecting and preserving the environment and the flora of the area.

r.31 – Protection of environment under – Obligation of – Held:

Rule 31 provides that every holder of a mining lease shall take all possible precautions for the protection of environment and control of pollution while conducting any mining operations in the area –

Air (Prevention and Control of Pollution) Act, 1981 – Environment (Protection) Act, 1986 – Water (Prevention and Control of Pollution) Act, 1974.

Notification/Circular:

Environment Impact Assessment (EIA) Notification dtd. 27th Jan. 1994 – Nature of – Held: It is a prohibitory notification and directs that on and from the date of its publication in the official gazette: (i) expansion or modernization of any activity (if pollution load is to exceed the existing one) and (ii) a new project listed in Schedule I to the notification, shall not be undertaken unless it has been accorded EC by the Central Government in accordance with the procedure specified in the notification – Further, EIA 1994 is also mandatory in character – It is applicable to all mining operations, new mining projects and renewal of mining leases –

Environment (Protection) Act, 1986 – ss.3(1), 3(2)(v) – Environment (Protection) Rules, 1986 – r.5(3)(d).

Environment Impact Assessment (EIA) Notification dtd. 27th Jan. 1994 – Grant under, of environment clearance (EC) – Purpose of – Held: On receipt of an EC a mining lease holder can extract a mineral only from a specified site, upto the sanctioned capacity and only for a period of five years from the date of grant of EC – Consequently, a mining lease holder would necessarily have to obtain a fresh EC every five years and can also apply for an increase in the sanctioned capacity – Environment.

Environment Impact Assessment (EIA) Notification dtd. 27th Jan. 1994 – Grant under, of EC – Operation of – Held: There is no concept of a retrospective EC – Its validity effectively starts only from the day it is granted – It takes precedence over the mining lease – Thus, mining operations under a mining lease are dependent on and 'subordinate' to the EC – Environment.

Environment Impact Assessment (EIA) Notification dtd. 27th Jan. 1994 – EC – Requirement of, for ongoing mining project – Exemption, when given – Held: An exemption is granted from the requirement of obtaining an EC if there is no expansion and the existing pollution load is not exceeded – However, a no objection certificate from the SPCB is necessary for continuing the mining operations – Environment.

Environment Impact Assessment (EIA) Notification dtd. 27th Jan. 1994 – Expansion and modernization of existing projects – Base year for considering pollution load while proposing any expansion activity – Determination of – Discussed – Environment.

Environment Impact Assessment (EIA) 14th September, 2006 –

Requirement under – Environment Clearance (EC) – Held: EIA 2006 required prior EC for projects or activities mentioned in the Schedule to it, both for major as well as minor minerals, if the leased area is 5 hectares or more – Environment.

Environment Impact Assessment (EIA) 14th September, 2006 –

Environment Clearance (EC) – Grant of – If retrospective – Held: An EC will come into force not earlier than the date of its grant – The concept of an ex post facto or a retrospective EC is completely alien to environmental jurisprudence – Environment.

Mines and Minerals:

Mining plan – Actual Production limit – Violations of – Held: A mining plan is valid for a period of five years – 20% deviation from the mining plan (in terms of over-production) would be easonable and permissible – A mining lease holder cannot extract the five year quantity (with a variation of 20%) in one or two years only.

Illegal Mining – What is – Plea of lessees that a mining operation only outside the mining lease area would constitute 'illegal mining' – Held: Not tenable – Illegal mining takes within its fold excess extraction of a mineral over the permissible limit even within the mining lease area which is held under lawful authority, if that excess extraction is contrary to the mining scheme, the mining plan, the mining lease or a statutory requirement – Mines and Minerals (Development and Regulation) Act, 1957 – s.23 C – Mineral Concession Rules, 1960 – r.2(iia) . Encroachment – Illegal mining outside the sanctioned mining areas – Direction issued. Consequences of Illegal mining – Discussed – Mines and Minerals (Development and

Regulation) Act, 1957 – s.21(5). Illegal mining – Penalty/Compensation for – Discussed – Mines and Minerals (Development and Regulation) Act, 1957 (MMDR) – s.21(5).

Forest (Conservation) Act, 1980 – s.2 – Violation of – Held: Since defaulting mining lease holders had paid additional Net Present Value (NPV) as well as an amount towards penal compensatory afforestation, it must be assumed that violation of the Act has been condoned to a limited extent – Environment.

Issuing directions, the Court

HELD:

Justice M.B. Shah Commission of Inquiry

1. The first report given by the Commission was a general, overall perspective on the subject, therefore, there is absolutely no question of any notice being issued to any mining lease holder under Section 8B or the right of cross examination being granted to any mining lease holder under Section 8C of the 1952 Act.

While the second report went into specific details of several mining lease holders –but herein one is not concerned with these specifics. Therefore, whether notices were or were not issued to the lease holders who were the subject matter of discussion in the second report is of no consequence. No irregularity or illegality has been committed so as to vitiate the first report. A resume of the procedure followed will indicate that full opportunity was given to the lease holders to have their say. [Paras 32-34, 43] [394-E; 398-A-B, D; 401-C-D]

• • •

CHAPTER XLII

SHAYARA BANO Vs. UNION OF INDIA AND OTHERS, AUGUST 22, 2017

Citations: [2017] 9 SCR 797, (2017) 9 SCC 1

[JAGDISH SINGH KHEHAR, CJI, KURIAN JOSEPH, R. F. NARIMAN, UDAY UMESH LALIT

AND S. ABDUL NAZEER, JJ.]

MAJORITY OPINION

Muslim Law: Talaq-e-biddat – The practice of Talaq-e-biddat is set aside. (Per Court) Muslim Law: Talaq-e-biddat – Triple Talaq by a Muslim husband which severs the marital bond – Constitutionality of – Held: In *Shamim Ara case, it was held that the correct law of Talaq as ordained by the Holy Quran is that, the Talaq must be for a reasonable cause and be preceded by attempts at reconciliation between the husband and the wife by two arbiters - one from the wife's family and the other from the husband's; if the attempts fail, Talaq may be effected" – Given the fact that Triple Talaq is instantaneous and irrevocable, it is obvious that any attempt at reconciliation between the husband and wife by two arbiters from their families, which is essential to save the marital tie, cannot ever take place – This form of Talaq is manifestly arbitrary in the sense that the marital tie can be broken capriciously and whimsically by a Muslim man without any attempt at reconciliation so as to save it – This form of Talaq must, therefore, be held to be violative of the fundamental right contained under Art.14 of the Constitution of India – Therefore, the 1937 Act, insofar as it seeks to recognize and enforce Triple Talaq, is within the meaning of the expression "laws in force" in Art.13(1) and must be struck down as being void to the extent that it recognizes and enforces Triple Talaq – Muslim Personal Laws (Shariat) Application Act, 1937 – s.2 – Constitution of India – Art.13(1). (Per Nariman, J.)

Muslim Law: Sunnis – Various sub-sects of Sunnis –

Discussed. (Per Nariman, J.)

Muslim Law: Various forms of divorce recognised in Islamic law – Discussed. (Per Nariman, J.) Muslim Law: Triple Talaq – Legal sanctity and constitutional protection – Triple Talaq is not an integral part of the religious practice – Merely because a practice has continued for long, that by itself cannot make it valid if it has been expressly declared to be impermissible – The whole purpose of the 1937 Act was to declare Shariat as the rule of decision and to discontinue anti-Shariat practices with respect to subjects enumerated in s.2 which include talaq – Therefore, in any case, after the introduction of the 1937 Act, no practice against the tenets of Quran is permissible – Therefore, there cannot be any Constitutional protection to such a practice – Constitution of India – Art.25 – Muslim Personal Laws (Shariat) Application Act, 1937 – s.2. (Per Kurian, J.)

Muslim Law: Whether what is wrong in Quran can be legally right – Held: What is held to be bad in the Holy Quran cannot be good in Shariat and, in that sense, what is bad in theology is bad in law as well. (Per Kurian, J.)

Constitution of India: Art.14 – When something is done by the legislature capriciously, irrationally and/or without adequate determining principle or which is excessive and disproportionate, such legislation would be manifestly arbitrary – Therefore, arbitrariness in the sense of manifest arbitrariness would apply to negate legislation as well under Art.14 – Applying the test of manifest arbitrariness, it is clear that Triple Talaq is a form of Talaq which is itself considered to be something innovative, namely, that it is not in the Sunna, being an irregular or heretical form of Talaq – Muslim law. (Per Nariman, J.)

Muslim Personal Laws (Shariat) Application Act, 1937: s.2 –

Whether the 1937 Act can be said to recognise and enforce Triple Talaq as a rule of law to be followed by the courts in India – Held:

The 1937 Act is a pre-constitutional legislative measure which would fall directly within Art.13(1) of the Constitution of India – True, the Objects and Reasons of a statute throw light on the backgroundin which the statute was enacted, but it is difficult to read the non-obstante clause of s.2 as governing the enacting part of the section – It is, therefore, clear that all forms of Talaq recognized and enforced by Muslim personal law are recognized and enforced by the 1937 Act – This would necessarily include Triple Talaq when it comes to the Muslim personal law applicable to Sunnis in India – s.2 recognizes or enforces Triple Talaq because the Section makes Triple Talaq "the rule of decision in cases where the parties are Muslims" – Thus, the 1937 Act is a law made by the legislature before the Constitution came into force, it would fall squarely within the expression "laws in force" in Art.13(3)(b) and would be hit by Art.13(1) if found to be inconsistent with the provisions of Part III of the Constitution, to the extent of such inconsistency – Constitution of India – Arts.13(1), 13(3)(b). (Per Nariman, J.)

Muslim Personal Laws (Shariat) Application Act, 1937: s.2 –

Law applicable to Muslim shall be only their personal law namely Shariat – It is not a legislation regulating Talaq – The 1937 Act simply makes Shariat applicable as the rule of decision in the matters enumerated in s.2 – Therefore, while Talaq is governed by Shariat, the specific grounds and procedure for Talaq have not been codified in the 1937 Act. (Per Kurian, J.)

Words and Phrases: Expression 'Shariat' – Meaning of. (Per Nariman, J.)

Words and Phrases: Shariat – Meaning of. (Per Kurian, J.)

MINORITY OPINION

Muslim Law: Talaq-e-biddat – Does the judgment of the Privy Council in the Rashid Ahmad case, upholding Talaq-e-biddat, require a relook – It was submitted, that after having acquired statutory status, the questions and subjects (including 'talaq-e-biddat'), would have to be in conformity (-and not in conflict), with the provisions of Part III – Fundamental Rights, of the Constitution – All these are important legal questions, requiring examination – The matter would certainly require a fresh look, because various High Courts, having examined the practice of divorce amongst Muslims, by way of 'talaqe-biddat', have arrived at the conclusion, that the judgment in the Rashid Ahmad case was rendered on an incorrect understanding, of the Muslim 'personal law' - 'Shariat'. (Per Khehar, CJI) Muslim law: Talaq-e-biddat – All the parties were unanimous, that despite the practice of 'talaq-e-biddat' being considered sinful, it was accepted amongst Sunni Muslims belonging to the Hanafi school, as valid in law, and has been in practice amongst them –

Talaq-e-biddat' is integral to the religious denomination of Sunnis belonging to the Hanafi school – The same is a part of their faith, having been followed for more than 1400 years, and as such, has to be accepted as being constituent of their 'personal law'. (Per Khehar, CJI) Muslim law: Talaq-e-biddat – Constitutionality under the Muslim 'personal law' - Shariat – The practice of 'talaq-e-biddat' being a constituent of 'personal law' has a stature equal to other fundamental rights, conferred in Part III of the Constitution – The practice cannot, therefore, be set aside, on the ground of being violative of the concept of the constitutional morality, through judicial intervention. (Per Khehar, CJI) Muslim law: Talaq-e-biddat – Need for legislation – It is not within the realm of judicial discretion, to set aside a matter of faith and religion – The position can only be salvaged by way of legislation – This is a case which presents a situation where the Court should exercise its discretion to issue appropriate directions under Article 142 of the Constitution – The Union of India is directed to consider appropriate legislation, particularly with reference to 'talaq-e-biddat' – Till such time as legislation in the matter is considered, Muslim husbands, are injuncted from pronouncing 'talaq-e-biddat' as a means for severing their matrimonial relationship. (Per Khehar, CJI)

Muslim Personal Law (Shariat) Application Act, 1937: It is incorrect statement that the questions/subjects covered by the Muslim Personal Law (Shariat) Application Act, 1937, ceased to be 'personal law', and got transformed into 'statutory law'. (Per Khehar, CJI)

Constitution of India: Art.25 and Arts. 14, 15 and 21 – 'Talaqe-biddat', does not violate the parameters expressed in Art.25 –

The practice is not contrary to public order, morality and health –

The practice also does not violate Arts.14, 15 and 21 of the Constitution, which are limited to State actions alone – Muslim law. (Per Khehar, CJI)

Constitution of India: Arts.25 and 44 r/w Seventh Schedule, List III, Entry 5 – Reforms to 'personal law' in India, with reference to socially unacceptable practices in different religions, have come about only by way of legislative intervention – Such legislative intervention is permissible under Arts.25(2) and 44, read with Entry 5 of the Concurrent List, contained in the Seventh Schedule of the Constitution – The said procedure alone need to be followed with reference to the practice of 'talaq-e-biddat', if the same is to be set aside. (Per Khehar, CJI)

International Conventions and Declarations: Binding effect for deciding validity of talaq-e-biddat – Held: Not binding since the practice of 'talaq-e-biddat', is a component of 'personal law', and has the protection of Art.25 of the Constitution. (Per Khehar, CJI)

Disposing of the matters, Held:

PER COURT: By a majority of 3 : 2, the practice of 'talaq-ebiddat' - triple talaq is set aside. [Para 1] [1158-B]

• • •

CHAPTER XLIII

JUSTICE K S PUTTASWAMY (RETD.) AND ANR. Vs. UNION OF INDIA AND ORS. AUGUST 24, 2017

Citations: [2017] 10 SCR 569, (2017) 10 SCC 1

[JAGDISH SINGH KHEHAR, CJI, J. CHELAMESWAR, S. A. BOBDE, R. K. AGRAWAL, R. F. NARIMAN,

ABHAY MANOHAR SAPRE, DR. D. Y. CHANDRACHUD, SANJAY KISHAN KAUL AND S. ABDUL NAZEER, JJ.]

Constitution of India – Art.21 – Right to privacy – Privacy is a constitutionally protected right in India – The decision in M. P. Sharma which holds that the right to privacy is not protected by the Constitution stands over-ruled – The decision in Kharak Singh to the extent that it holds that the right to privacy is not protected by the Constitution stands over-ruled – Right to privacy is protected as an intrinsic part of the right to life and personal liberty under Art.21 and as a part of the freedom guaranteed by Part III of the Constitution – Aadhar (Targeted Delivery of Financial and other Subsidies, Benefits and Services) Act, 2016. (Per Court) The Constitution is a sacred living document and, hence susceptible to appropriate interpretation of its provisions based on changing needs of the society – While interpreting any provision of the Constitution, the Preamble to the Constitution may be relied on as a remedy for mischief or/ and to find out the true meaning of the relevant provision as the case may be.

A scheme was propounded by the Government of India popularly known as the Aadhar card scheme. Under the said scheme, the Government of India collects and compiles both demographic and biometric data of the residents of this country to be used for various purposes. In the instant reference, the ground of attack on the said scheme is that the very collection of such data is violative of the "Right to Privacy". The issue reaches out to the foundation of a constitutional culture based on the protection of human rights and presents challenges for constitutional interpretation. Answering the reference, the Court

HELD: PER COURT:

(i) The decision in M.P. Sharma which holds that the right to privacy is not protected by the Constitution stands overruled;

(ii) The decision in Kharak Singh to the extent that it holds that the right to privacy is not protected by the Constitutions stands over-ruled;

(iii) The right to privacy is protected as an intrinsic part of the right to life and personal liberty under Article 21 and as a part of the freedoms guaranteed by Part III of the Constitution; (iv) Decisions subsequent to Kharak Singh which have enunciated the position in (iii) above lay down the correct

position in law. [Para 2][998-G-H; 999-A-B]

• • •

CHAPTER XLIV

COMMON CAUSE (A REGD. SOCIETY) Vs. UNION OF INDIA & ANOTHER, MARCH 09, 2018

Citations: [2018] 6 SCR 1, 2018 (5) SCC 1

[DIPAK MISRA, CJI, A. K. SIKRI, DR. D. Y. CHANDRACHUD, ASHOK BHUSHAN AND

A. M. KHANWILKAR, JJ.]

Constitution - Right to Self Determination - Article 21 of Constitution of India - Present petition filed seeking declaration that right to die with dignity be declared fundamental right within right to live with dignity under Article 21 of Constitution - Whether person be allowed to remain in stage of incurable passivity suffering or treating utterance of death as rhetoric - Whether law permits accelerating process of dying sans suffering when life is on inevitable decay - Whether right to life under Article 21 of Constitution includes right to die

Held while allowing the appeal,

In view of our conclusions as noted above the writ petition is allowed in the following manner:

(a) The right to die with dignity as fundamental right has already been declared by the Constitution Bench judgment of this Court in Gian Kaur case (supra) which we reiterate.

(b) We declare that an adult human being having mental capacity to take an informed decision has right to refuse medical treatment including withdrawal from life saving devices.

(c) A person of competent mental faculty is entitled to execute an advance medical directive in accordance with safeguards as referred to above.

Before we conclude, we acknowledge our indebtness to all the learned Advocates who have rendered valuable assistance with great industry and ability which made it possible for us to resolve issues of seminal public importance. We record our fullest appreciation for the assistance rendered by each and every counsel in this case.

• • •

CHAPTER XLV

MUNICIPAL CORPORATION, UJJAIN & ANR. Vs. BVG INDIA LIMITED AND ORS. MARCH 27, 2018

Citations: [2018] 6 SCR 861, [2018 (5) SCC 462]

[RANJAN GOGOI, R. BANUMATHI AND MOHAN M. SHANTANAGOUDAR, JJ.]

Tenders – Appellant-Corporation issued NIT for appointment of agency to carry out "Municipal Solid Waste Door to Door Collection and Transportation" – Bids were invited following a two-envelope system i.e. a technical bid and a financial bid – Technical bids of the parties were analysed thoroughly by a technical expert and marks were awarded as per specifications of the NIT –

Global Waste Management Cell Private Limited (GWMC) scored highest marks based on technical and financial weighted scores and hence was awarded the contract – Aggrieved, the unsuccessful bidder (respondent no.1) filed writ petition – High Court allowed the same and set aside the contract awarded in favour of GWMC –

On appeal, held: As a decision was qualitatively arrived at by the technical expert respondent no.2, the High Court need not have gone into the merits of such decision as an appellate authority, especially when there was no bias or malafide – There was no illegality, arbitrariness, irrationality or unreasonableness on the part of the expert body while in action – Moreover, the decision was taken keeping in mind the public interest and work experience of the successful bidder – In absence of any document evidencing the experience in the field in question in favour of respondent no.1, the High Court was not right in increasing the marks under the head of number of years of experience and expertise – High Court was also not justified in increasing the marks for responsiveness, as respondent no.1 had suppressed the fact that it had received show cause notices from various municipal corporations and thus, High Court ignored the element of public interest involved in the matter – Further, the method for evaluation of the financial bid as applied by the High Court was also not proper and was illogical, which led to unreasonableness and travesty of justice – Solid Waste Management Rules, 2016 – r.22.

Tenders – Judicial review of administrative decisions – Held:

The judicial review of administrative action is intended to prevent arbitrariness – The purpose of judicial review of administrative action is to check whether the choice or decision is made lawfully and not to check whether the choice or decision is sound – If the process adopted or decision made by the authority is not mala fide and not intended to favour someone; if the process adopted or decision made is neither so arbitrary nor irrational that under the facts of the case it can be concluded that no responsible authority acting reasonably and in accordance with relevant law could have reached such a decision; and if the public interest is not affected, there should be no interference u/Art.226 – Constitution of India – Art.226.

Tenders – Whether under the scope of judicial review, the High Court could ordinarily question the judgment of the expert consultant on the issue of technical qualifications of a bidder when the consultant takes into consideration various factors including the basis of non-performance of the bidder – Held: Under the scope of judicial review, the High Court could not ordinarily interfere with the judgment of the expert consultant on the issues of technical qualifications of a bidder when the consultant takes into consideration various factors including the basis of nonperformance of the bidder – The power of judicial review can be exercised only if there is unreasonableness, irrationality or arbitrariness and in order to avoid bias and mala fides.

Tenders – Whether a bidder who submits a bid expressly declaring that it is submitting the same independently and without any partners, consortium or joint venture can rely upon the technical qualifications of any third party for its qualification –

Held:

Tenders – Whether the High Court can independently evaluate the technical bids and financial bids of the parties, as an appellate authority, for coming to the conclusion – Held: It is not open to the Court to independently evaluate the technical bids and financial bids of the parties as an appellate authority for coming to its conclusion inasmuch as unless the thresholds of mala fides, intention to favour someone or bias, arbitrariness, irrationality or perversity are met, where a decision is taken purely on public interest, the Court ordinarily should exercise judicial restraint.

• • •

CHAPTER XLVI

SHAKTI VAHINI Vs. UNION OF INDIA AND OTHERS. MARCH 27, 2018

Citations: [2018] 3 SCR 770, (2018) 7 SCC 192

[DIPAK MISRA, CJI, A. M. KHANWILKAR AND DR. D. Y. CHANDRACHUD, JJ.]

Honour Crimes:

Writ petition – Seeking directions to State Governments and Central Government to take preventive steps to combat honour crimes; to submit State and National Plan of Action to curb such crimes; and seeking direction to the State Governments to constitute special cells and to launch prosecution in such cases – Held: Any kind of torture or torment or ill-treatment in the name of honour that tantamounts to atrophy of choice of an individual relating to love and marriage by any assembly, whatsoever nomenclature it assumes, is illegal and cannot be allowed – Consent of the family or the community or the clan is not necessary, once two adult individuals agree to enter into a wedlock – It is manifestation of their choice which is recognized u/Arts. 19 and 21 of the Constitution – Such constitutional right cannot succumb to the conception of class honour – Any infringement of such right is constitutional violation – Khap Panchayat or such assembly should not take the law into their hands and further cannot assume the character of the law implementing agency – Law has to be allowed to sustain by law enforcement agencies – Honour killings are condemned as a serious human rights violation – Therefore, it is recommended to the legislature to bring law appositely covering the field of honour killing – To meet the challenges of agonising affect of honour crime, there has to be preventive, remedial and punitive measures and hence the executive and administration of the States to add further measures to evolve a robust mechanism to the stated purpose – Constitution of India – Arts 19 and 21.

Words and Phrases:

'Khap panchayat' – Meaning of Disposing of the Writ Petition, the Court

HELD: 1. Class honour, howsoever perceived, cannot smother the choice of an individual which he or she is entitled to enjoy under compassionate Constitution of India. And this right of enjoyment of liberty deserves to be continually and zealously guarded so that it can thrive with strength and flourish with resplendence. The old order has to give way to the new. Feudal perception has to melt into oblivion paving the smooth path for liberty. [Para 1] [777-H; 778-A-B]

• • •

CHAPTER XLVII

NAVTEJ SINGH JOHAR & ORS. Vs. UNION OF INDIA THR. SECRETARY MINISTRY OF LAW AND JUSTICE, SEPTEMBER 06, 2018

Citations: [2018] 7 SCR 379, (2018) 10 SCC 1

[DIPAK MISRA, CJI, R. F. NARIMAN, A. M. KHANWILKAR, DR. D.Y. CHANDRACHUD AND

INDU MALHOTRA, JJ.]

Constitution - Validity of provision - Section 377 of Indian Penal Code, 1860 (IPC) and Articles 14, 15, 19, and 21 of Constitution of India, 1950 - Writ Petition was filed for declaring "right to sexuality", "right to sexual autonomy" and "right to choice of a sexual partner" to be part of the right to life guaranteed Under Article 21 of Constitution of India and further to declare Section 377 of IPC to be unconstitutional - Whether Section 377 of IPC as it criminalises consensual sexual acts of adults (i.e. persons above the age of 18 years who were competent to consent) in private, was violative of Articles 14, 15, 19, and 21 of Constitution.

Writ Petition was filed for declaring "right to sexuality", "right to sexual autonomy" and "right to choice of a sexual partner" to be part of the right to life guaranteed under Article 21 of the Constitution of India and further to declare Section 377 of IPC to be unconstitutional. It is urged by the learned Counsel for the Petitioners that individuals belonging to the LGBT group suffer discrimination and abuse throughout their lives due to the existence of Section 377 of IPC which is nothing but a manifestation of a mindset of societal values prevalent during the Victorian era where sexual activities were considered mainly for procreation. The said community remains in a constant state of fear which is not conducive for their growth. It is contended that they suffer at the hands of law and are also deprived of the citizenry rights which are protected under the Constitution. Petitioners face a violation of their fundamental rights to an extent which is manifestly clear and it is a violation which strikes at the very root or substratum of their existence. The discrimination suffered at the hands of the majority, the onslaught to their dignity and invasion on the right to privacy is demonstrably visible and permeates every nook and corner of the society. It is the argument of the Petitioners that Section 377, if retained in its present form, would involve the violation of, not one but, several fundamental rights of the LGBTs, namely, right to privacy, right to dignity, equality, liberty and right to freedom of expression. The Petitioners contend that sexual orientation which is a natural corollary of gender identity is protected under Article 21 of the Constitution and any discrimination meted out to the LGBT community on the basis of sexual orientation would run counter to the mandate provided under the Constitution and the said view has also gained approval of this Court in the NALSA case.

Held, while allowing the petitions:

i. In view of the aforesaid findings, it is declared that insofar as Section 377 criminalises consensual sexual acts of adults (i.e. persons above the age of 18 years who are competent to consent) in private, is violative of Articles 14, 15, 19, and 21 of the Constitution.

It is, however, clarified that such consent must be free consent, which is completely voluntary in nature, and devoid of any duress or coercion.

ii. The declaration of the aforesaid reading down of Section 377 shall not, however, lead to the reopening of any concluded prosecutions, but can certainly be relied upon in all pending matters whether they are at the trial, appellate, or revisional stages.

iii. The provisions of Section 377 will continue to govern non-consensual sexual acts against adults, all acts of carnal intercourse against minors, and acts of bestiality.

• • •

CHAPTER XLVIII

JUSTICE K. S. PUTTASWAMY (RETD.) & ANR. Vs. UNION OF INDIA & ORS. SEPTEMBER 26, 2018

Citations: [2018] 8 SCR 1, (2019) 1 SCC 1

[DIPAK MISRA, CJI, A. K. SIKRI, A. M. KHANWILKAR, DR. D. Y. CHANDRACHUD AND ASHOK BHUSHAN, JJ.]

Constitution - Aadhaar scheme - Right to privacy - Articles 14,19,21,110 and 110(1) of Constitution of India and Sections 7,28(5),29,29(1),29(2),33,47,57,59 of The Aadhaar Act, 2016 - Present petitions filed challenging constitutional validity of Aadhaar Act, 2016 and executive's Scheme notified by Government, by which Unique Identification Authority of India (UIDAI) was constituted to implement UIDAI Scheme - In writ petitions scheme had primarily been challenged on ground that it violates fundamental rights of innumerable citizens of India, namely, right to privacy falling under Article 21 of Constitution of India - Whether provisions of Aadhaar Act, 2016 was liable to be struck down as violative of constitution.

Held while disposing of the appeal,

We have noticed above that according to Aadhaar Act Section 33 disclosure of information can be made as per Sub-section (1) pursuant to an order of Court, not inferior to that of District Judge. The order directing for disclosure of information having been passed by Judicial Magistrate First Class, in the present case, the order is not in consonance with Sub-section (1) of Section 33, hence the order passed by Judicial Magistrate, First Class dated 22.10.2013 and order of the High Court passed in reference to the said order deserves to be set aside. Criminal Appeal is allowed accordingly.

1178. No case is made out to initiate any contempt proceedings in the contempt applications as prayed for. All the contempt petitions are dismissed.

1179. In result, this batch of cases is decided in following manner:

(i) All the Writ Petitions filed Under Article 32 as well as Transfer Cases are disposed of as per our conclusions recorded above.

(ii) Criminal Appeal arising out of S.L.P. (Criminal) No. 2524 of 2014 is allowed.

(iii) All the contempt applications are closed.

1180. Before we part, we record our deep appreciation for the industry, hard work and eloquence shown by learned Counsel for the parties appearing before us, which was amply demonstrated in their respective arguments. Learned Counsel have enlightened us with all relevant concerned materials available in this country and abroad. The concern raised by these Public Interest Litigations is a concern shown for little Indian for whom the Society, Government and Court exists. We appreciate the concern and passion expressed before us by learned Counsel appearing for both the parties as well as those, who were permitted to intervene in the matter. We close by once more recording of our appreciation for the cause espoused in these cases.

• • •

CHAPTER XLIX

JARNAIL SINGH & OTHERS Vs. LACHHMI NARAIN GUPTA & OTHERS, SEPTEMBER 26, 2018

Citations: [2018] 10 SCR 663, (2018) 10 SCC-396

[DIPAK MISRA, CJI, KURIAN JOSEPH, R. F. NARIMAN, SANJAY KISHAN KAUL AND INDU MALHOTRA, JJ.]

Constitution of India – Arts.16(4-A), 16(4-B), 335, 341 and 342 – Interpretation of – Reservation in promotion – Judgment in M. Nagaraj case – Correctness of – Referred to five judge Constitution Bench – Held: Judgment in M. Nagaraj case does not need to be referred to seven–Judge Bench – However, the conclusion in M. Nagaraj case that the State has to collect quantifiable data showing backwardness of the Scheduled Castes and the Scheduled Tribes, being contrary to the nine-Judge Bench in Indra Sawhney

(1) case, is held to be invalid to this extent. Constitution of India – Reservation – Principle of Creamy Layer – Application to Schedules Castes (SCs) and Scheduled Tribes (STs) – Held: When a Court applies the creamy layer principle to SCs and STs, it does not in any manner tinker with the Presidential List u/Arts. 341 or 342 – Caste or group or sub-group named in the said List continues exactly as before – It is only those persons within that group or sub-group, who have come out of untouchability or backwardness by virtue of belonging to the creamy layer, who are excluded from the benefit of reservation. Constitution of India – Arts.14 and 16(1) – Reservation – Principle of Creamy Layer – Held: Creamy Layer Principle sounds in Arts. 14 and 16(1), as unequal within the same class are being treated equally with other members of that class.

Interpretation of Statutes – Harmonious Interpretation – Held:

Arts. 14 and 16 when harmoniously interpreted along with Arts.341 and 342, makes it clear that Parliament has complete freedom to include or exclude persons from the Presidential Lists based on relevant factors – Constitution of India – Arts. 14, 16, 341 and 342.

Constitution of India – Reservation – Object of – Held: Whole object of reservation is to see that backward classes of citizens move forward so that they may march hand in hand with other citizens of India on an equal basis – This will not be possible if only the creamy layer within a class bag all the coveted jobs in the public sector and perpetuate themselves, leaving the rest of the class as backward as they always were.

• • •

CHAPTER L

JOSEPH SHINE Vs. UNION OF INDIA, SEPTEMBER 27, 2018

Citations: [2018] 11 SCR 765, (2019) 3 SCC 39

[DIPAK MISRA, CJI, R.F. NARIMAN, A.M. KHANWILKAR, DR. D.Y. CHANDRACHUD AND

INDU MALHOTRA, JJ.]

Penal Code, 1860: s.497 – s. 198 of Cr.P.C – Offence of Adultery – Whether unconstitutional, being violative of Articles 14, 15 and 21 – Held: (Per Court): s. 497 IPC and s. 198 Cr.P.C. being violative of Articles 14, 15 and 21 of the Constitution, are unconstitutional – (Per Dipak Misra, CJI): s. 497 treats women, subordinate to men – The rationale of the provision suffers from absence of logicality of approach and therefore suffers from vice of Art. 14 being manifestly arbitrary – Section 497 also creates invidious distinctions based on gender stereotypes which creates a dent in the individual dignity of women and hence offends Art. 21 –

Offence of adultery u/s. 497 IPC does not fit into the concept of crime – If it is treated as a crime, there would be immense intrusion into the extreme privacy of the matrimonial sphere – Section 198 Cr.P.C. deals with procedure for filing complaint in relation to offence u/s. 497 IPC, and hence it is also unconstitutional – (Per R.F. Nariman, J.): What is punished as 'adultery' is not 'adultery' per se, but the proprietary interest of a married man in his wife –

The archaic law u/s. 497 has long outlived its purpose and does not square with today's constitutional morality – It has become utterly irrational, manifestly arbitrary and discriminatory and hence violative of Art. 14 and 15(1) – Dignity of individual is a facet of Art. 21 – A statutory provision which degrades the status of women, falls foul of modern constitutional doctrine and must be struck down being violative of Art. 21 – Section 198 Cr.P.C. also being discriminatory provision, is held constitutionally infirm – (Per Chandrachud, J:): Right to sexual autonomy and privacy has been granted the stature of a constitutional right – Section 497, in its effort to protect the sanctity of marriage, has adopted a notion of marriage which does not regard the man and the woman as equal partners – Section 497 thus subordinates the woman to a position of inferiority

– Constitutional morality requires the court to enforce constitutional guarantees of equality before law, non-discrimination on account of sex and dignity, all of which are affected by operation of s. 497 – Therefore, s. 497 IPC violates Art. 14 – It is based on gender stereotypes about the role of women and violates the nondiscrimination principle embodied in Art. 15 – It is also a denial of the constitutional guarantees of dignity, liberty, privacy and sexual autonomy which are intrinsic to Art. 21 – Thus, Section 497 IPC is unconstitutional – (Per Indu Malhotra, J.): Section 497 IPC fails to consider both men and women as equally autonomous individuals in society – The anomalies and inconsistencies in s. 497 IPC would render the provision liable to be struck down on the ground of being arbitrary and discriminatory – Any legislation which treats similarly situated persons unequally or discriminates between persons on the basis of sex alone is liable to be struck down as being violative of Articles 14 and 15 – Right to privacy u/Art. 21 would include the right of two adults to enter into a sexual relationship outside marriage – An invasion of privacy u/Art. 21, by the State must meet a three-fold requirement i.e. (i) legality, (ii) need and (iii) proportionality – Section 497 IPC as it stands today fails to meet the three fold requirement and therefore violative of Art. 21 – Section 198(2) of Cr.P.C. which contains the procedure for prosecution under Chapter XX of IPC shall be unconstitutional only to the extent that it is applicable to the offence of adultery u/s. 497 IPC –

Constitution of India – Arts. 14, 15 and 21.

Constitution of India: Art. 15(3) – Protective discrimination – Applicability of – To s.497 IPC – Held (Per: R.F. Nariman, J.): Art. 15(3) is applicable only to the law made by the State after coming into force of the Constitution and not to "existing law" – s. 497 is, in constitutional language, an "existing law" which continues, by virtue of Art. 372(1), to apply, and could not be said to be law made by the "State" – (Per D.Y. Chandrachud, J.): - Art. 15 (3) does not protect a statutory provision that entrenches patriarchal notions in garb of protecting women – 'Protection' afforded to women u/s. 497 highlights the lack of sexual agency that the Section imputes to a woman – (Per: Indu Malhotra, J.): – The purpose of Art. 15(3) is to further socio-economic equality of women – Section 497 cannot be considered to be beneficial legislation covered by Art. 15(3) –

Penal Code, 1860 – s. 497.

Art. 21 – Right to privacy and personal liberty – Held: (Per Indu Malhotra, J.): An invasion of privacy u/Art. 21, by the State must be justified on the basis of a law that is reasonable and valid – Such invasion must meet three-fold requirement i.e. (i) legality, (ii) need and (iii) proportionality – Section 497 of IPC fails to meet the three-fold requirement – Therefore, right to privacy u/Art.21 would include the right of two adults to enter into a sexual relationship outside marriage – Penal Code, 1860 – s. 497.

Art. 21 – Right to live with dignity – Scope of – Held: (Per: Indu Malhotra, J.): – Right to live with dignity includes the right not to be subjected to public censure and punishment by the State except where absolutely necessary – Penal Code, 1860 – s. 497.

Criminal Law:

Criminal sanction – When justified – Held:(Per: Indu Malhotra, J.) – Criminal sanction may be justified where there is a public element in the wrong – State must follow the minimalist approach in the criminalization of offences, keeping in view the respect for the autonomy of the individual to make his/her personal choices – Adultery is only a moral wrong qua the spouse and the family – In order to determine what conduct requires State interference through criminal sanction, the State must consider whether civil remedy will serve the purpose – Where civil remedy for a wrongful act is sufficient, it may not warrant criminal sanction by the State – Penal Code, 1860 – s. 497 – Remedy.

Presumption:

Presumption of constitutionality – Held: (Per Indu Malhotra, J.) – There would be no presumption of constitutionality in a pre-constitutional law – Constitutionalism.

Legislation:

Purpose of legislation – Held (Per Dipak Misra, CJI) – A legislation should serve and promote good life – It should be fit and equitable so that it can have a right to command obedience.

Law:

Constitutionality of procedural law – When substantive provision is held unconstitutional – Held (Per Dipak Misra, CJI) When the substantive provision goes, the procedural provision has to to pave the same path.

Doctrine/Principle:

Principle of Conventure – Explained.

Maxim:

'Cessante ratione legis, cessat ipsa lex' – Applicability of.

Words & Phrases:

'Adultery' – Meaning of.

'Crime' – Meaning of.

• • •

CHAPTER LI

COMPETITION COMMISSION OF INDIA Vs. BHARTI AIRTEL LIMITED AND OTHERS, DECEMBER 05, 2018

Citations: [2018] 14 SCR 489, (2019) 2 SCC 521

[A. K. SIKRI AND ASHOK BHUSHAN, JJ.]

Competition Act, 2002: ss.14, 19, 21, 21A and 26 – RJIL filed information under the Act alleging anti-competitive agreement/ cartel having been formed by three major telecom operators (IDOs) along with COAI – Grievance of RJIL was that the IDOs intentionally ignored its request to augment Point of Interconnection (POIs) for access, National Long Distance and international Long Distance services, as the capacity already provided to it was causing huge POI congestion resulting in call failures on its network – Apart from IDOs, certain allegations were made against COAI also – It was alleged that IDOs were denying mobile number portability (MNP) requests of customers who wanted to switch to RJIL competing service and that COAI was acting at the behest of IDOs against the interest of competing member i.e. RJIL and not for the common interest of industry and consumers as a whole – CCI held that prima facie case existed and an investigation was warranted and directed Director General to cause investigation in the case – Jurisdiction of CCI to deal with the matter was challenged by IDOs and COAI –

Held: As the TRAI is constituted as an expert regulatory body which specifically governs the telecom sector, the said aspects of the disputes are to be decided by the TRAI in the first instance – These are jurisdictional aspects – TRAI, being a specialised sectoral regulator and also armed with sufficient power to ensure fair, nondiscriminatory and competitive market in the telecom sector, is better suited to decide the said issues – The concepts of "subscriber", "test period", "reasonable demand", "test phase and commercial phase rights and obligations", "reciprocal obligations of service providers" or "breaches of any contract and/or practice", arising out of TRAI Act and the policy so declared, are the matters within the jurisdiction of the Authority/TDSAT under the TRAI Act only –

Once that exercise is done and there are findings returned by the TRAI which lead to prima facie conclusion that IDOs have indulged in anti-competitive practices, CCI can be activated to investigate the matter going by the criteria laid down in relevant provisions of Competition Act – Telecom Regulatory Authority of India Act, 1997 – Telegraph Act, 1885 – Telecommunication – Jurisdiction. Competition Act, 2002: Salient features of the Act, discussed. Competition Act, 2002: Competition Commission of India (CCI) – Duties and functions – The CCI is entrusted with duties, powers and functions to deal with three kinds of anti-competitive practices – These are: (a) where agreements are entered into by certain persons with a view to cause an appreciable adverse effect on competition; (b) where any enterprise or group of enterprises, which enjoys dominant position, abuses the said dominant position; and (c) regulating the combination of enterprises by means of mergers or amalgamations to ensure that such mergers or amalgamations do not become anti-competitive or abuse the dominant position which they can attain – The purpose of CCI is to eliminate such practices which are having adverse effect on the competition, to promote and sustain competition and to protect the interest of the consumers and ensure freedom of trade, carried on by the other participants, in India – For the purpose of conducting an inquiry, the CCI is empowered to call any person for rendering assistance and/or produce the records/material for arriving at even the prima facie opinion.

Competition Act, 2002: s.26(1) – Writ petition against order under s.26(1) of 2002 Act – Maintainability of – RJIL filed information under the Act alleging anti-competitive agreement/cartel having been formed by three major telecom operators (IDOs) along with COAI – CCI exercised its right under s.26 and held that prima facie case existed and an investigation was warranted into the matter and directed Director General to cause investigation in the case –

In writ petition, High Court was called upon to decide as to whether the jurisdiction of the CCI was entirely excluded or to what extent the CCI could exercise its jurisdiction in these cases when the matter could be dealt with any another regulator, namely, the TRAI – Held: When such jurisdictional issues arose, the writ petition would clearly be maintainable – Constitution of India – Art.226 – Judicial review. Competition Act, 2002: s.26(1) – Whether the High Court could give its findings on merits – Held: Once the order under s.26(1) of the 2002 Act is held to be administrative in nature and that it was merely a prima facie opinion directing the Director

General to carry the investigation, the High Court was not competent to adjudge the validity of such an order on merits – The observations of the High Court giving findings on merits, therefore, were not appropriate – At the same time, since the order of the High Court is upheld on the aspect that the CCI could exercise jurisdiction only after proceedings under the TRAI Act had concluded/attained finality, the ultimate direction given by the High Court quashing the order passed by the CCI is not liable to be interfered with as such an exercise carried out by the CCI was premature.

Telecom Regulatory Authority of India Act, 1997: Salient features of the Act, discussed.

• • •

CHAPTER LII

SWISS RIBBONS PVT. LTD. & ANR. Vs. UNION OF INDIA & ORS. JANUARY 25, 2019

Citations: [2019] 3 SCR 535, (2019) 4 SCC 17

[R. F. NARIMAN AND NAVIN SINHA, JJ.]

Insolvency and Bankruptcy Code, 2016:

Constitutional validity of – Held: Provisions of the Code passes constitutional muster.

ss. 5(7), 5(8), 5(20), 7(1), 7(4), 7(5), 8 and 9 – Classification between financial creditor and operational creditor – Whether discriminatory, arbitrary, and violative of Art. 14 – Held: Preserving the corporate debtor as a going concern, while ensuring maximum recovery for all creditors being the objective of the Code, financial creditors are clearly different from operational creditors – Thus, there is an intelligible differentia between the two which has a direct relation to the objects sought to be achieved by the Code – Thus, there is no discrimination – Constitution of India – Art. 14. ss. 3, 3(9)(c), 214(e), 60, 65, 75, 7, 8 and 9 – Notice, hearing, and set-off or counterclaim qua financial debts – Triggering of insolvency resolution process by financial creditors and operation creditors – Submission that the difference in the triggering process at behest of financial creditors and operational creditors is discriminatory and arbitrary – Held: A financial creditor has to prove "default" as opposed to an operational creditor who merely" claims" a right to payment of a liability or obligation in respect of a debt which may be due – In view thereof, the differentiation in the triggering of insolvency resolution process by financial creditors u/s. 7 and by operational creditors u/ss. 8 and 9 becomes clear –

Insolvency and Bankruptcy Board of India (Information Utilities) Regulations, 2017 – Insolvency and Bankruptcy (Application to Adjudicating Authority) Rules, 2016 – Form I. ss. 21, 24, 28 and 30(2)(b) r/w s. 31 – Operational creditors – Right to vote in the committee of creditors – Plea that operational creditor do not have even a single vote in committee of creditors –

Held: Financial creditors are best equipped to assess viability and feasibility of the business of the corporate debtor and evaluate the contents of a resolution plan – On the other hand, operational creditors, who provide goods and services, are involved only in recovering amounts that are paid for such goods and services, and are typically unable to assess viability and feasibility of business – Resolution plan cannot pass muster u/s. 30(2)(b) rw s. 31 unless a minimum payment is made to operational creditors, being not less than liquidation value – Regulation 38 strengthens the rights of operational creditors by statutorily incorporating the principle of fair and equitable dealing of operational creditors' rights, together with priority in payment over financial creditors – Thus, the operational creditors are not discriminated against nor Art. 14 has been infracted either on the ground of equals being treated unequally or on the ground of manifest arbitrariness – Insolvency and Bankruptcy Board of India (Insolvency Resolution Process for Corporate Persons) Regulations, 2016 – Regulation 38 –

Constitution of India – Art. 14.

ss.12A(as amended) and 60 – s. 12A wherein withdrawal of application admitted u/ss 7, 9 or 10, with approval of ninety per cent voting shares of the committee of creditors – s. 12A if violative of Art. 14 – Held: s. 12A is not violative of Art. 14 – ILC Report has explained that as all financial creditors have to put their heads together to allow such withdrawal as, ordinarily, an omnibus settlement involving all creditors ought, ideally, to be entered into – In any case, the figure of ninety per cent, in the absence of anything further to show that it is arbitrary, must pertain to the domain of legislative policy – Also, if the committee of creditors arbitrarily rejects a just settlement and/or withdrawal claim, the NCLT, and thereafter, the NCLAT can always set aside such decision u/s. 60 – Insolvency and Bankruptcy (Second Amendment) Act, 2018 –

Insolvency and Bankruptcy Board of India (Insolvency Resolution Process for Corporate Persons) Regulations, 2016 – Reg 30A. s. 210 – Private Information Utilities – Evidence provided by private information utilities – Plea that Private Information Utilities not governed by proper norms and evidence of loan default in records of such utility not conclusive evidence – Held: Regulations 20 and 21 makes it clear that apart from the stringent requirements as to registration of such utility, the moment information of default is received, such information has to be communicated to all parties and sureties to the debt and an information utility shall expeditiously undertake the process of authentication and verification of information – Evidence provided by private information utilities is only prima facie evidence of default which is rebuttable by the corporate debtor – Insolvency and Bankruptcy Board of India (Insolvency

Resolution Process for Corporate Persons) Regulations, 2016 – Regulations 20 and 21

ss. 18, 41, 42 and 28 – Resolution professional – Adjudicatory power, under the Code and the Regulations – Held: It is clear from the Code as well as the Regulations that the resolution professional has no adjudicatory powers – Resolution professional is given administrative as opposed to quasi-judicial powers – Even when the resolution professional is to make a "determination" under Regulation 35A, he is only to apply to the Adjudicating Authority for appropriate relief based on the determination made – Thus, the resolution professional is really a facilitator of the resolution process, whose administrative functions are overseen by the committee of creditors and by the Adjudicating Authority – Insolvency and Bankruptcy Board of India (Insolvency Resolution Process for Corporate Persons) Regulations, 2016 – Regulations 10, 12, 13, 14, and 35A. s. 29A(as amended) – Retrospective application – Submission that vested rights of erstwhile promoters to participate in the recovery process of a corporate debtor have been impaired by retrospective application of s. 29A – Held: A statute is not retrospective merely because it affects existing rights or merely because a part of the requisites for its action is drawn from a time antecedent to its passing – Resolution applicant has no vested right for consideration or approval of its resolution plan – By application of s. 29A, no vested right is taken away – Since a resolution applicant who applies u/ s. 29A(c) has no vested right to apply for being considered as a resolution applicant, submission cannot be accepted.

s. 29A and s.35(1)(f) proviso – s. 29A if restricted to malfeasance – Submission that s. 29A puts a blanket ban on participation of all promoters of corporate debtors, without any mechanism to weed out the unscrupulous as against the efficient manager but who have not been able to pay off their debts due to other reasons – Held: s. 29A not restricted to malfeasance – Legislative purpose which permeates s. 29A continues to permeate the Section when it applies not merely to resolution applicants, but to liquidation also.

s. 29(A)(c) – One-year period in s. 29A – Non-performing asset – Plea that u/s. 29A(c), a person's account may be classified as a non- performing asset even though he is not a willful defaulter; and that the period of one year referred in clause (c) is wholly arbitrary and without any basis either in rationality or in law –

Held: A person is a defaulter when an installment and/or interest on the principal remains overdue for more than three months, after which, its account is declared NPA – During the period of one year thereafter, this grace period is given to such person to pay off the debt – If a person is unable to repay a loan taken, in whole or in part, within this period of one year and three months, he would be ineligible to become a resolution applicant – This legislative policy cannot be found fault with – Neither can the period of one year be found fault with. ss. 29A(j) and 5(24A) – Related party – Plea that persons who may be relatives of erstwhile promoters are debarred from becoming a resolution applicant – Held: Persons who act jointly or in concert with others are connected with the business activity of the resolution applicant – Similarly, all the categories of persons mentioned in s. 5(24A) show that such persons must be "connected" with the resolution applicant within the meaning of s. 29A(j) – Thus, the said categories of persons who are collectively mentioned under the caption "relative" obviously need to have a connection with the business activity of the resolution applicant – In the absence of showing that such person is "connected" with the business of the Activity of the resolution applicant, such person cannot possibly be disqualified u/s. 29A(j) – Explanation I clause (ii) to s. 29A(j) makes it clear that if a person is otherwise covered as a "connected person", this provision would also cover a person who is in management or control of the business of the corporate debtor during the implementation of a resolution plan – Thus, any such person is not indeterminate at all, but is a person who is in the saddle of the business of the corporate debtor either at an anterior point of time or even during implementation of the resolution plan.

s. 29A – Exemption of micro, small and medium enterprises from s. 29A – Justification of – Held: Justified – Rationale for excluding such industries from the eligibility criteria laid down in ss. 29A(c) and 29A(h) is because qua such industries, other resolution applicants may not be forthcoming, which then will inevitably lead not to resolution, but to liquidation – Micro, Small and Medium Enterprises Development Act, 2006 – s. 7.

s. 53 – Distribution of assets – Submission that in the event of liquidation, operational creditors would never get anything as they rank below all other creditors, including other unsecured creditors who happen to be financial creditors, thus s. 53(1)(f) discriminatory and arbitrary thus, violative of Art. 14 – Held: s. 53 does not violate

Art. 14 – Repayment of financial debts infuses capital into the economy inasmuch as banks and financial institutions are able, with the money that has been paid back, to further lend such money to other entrepreneurs for their businesses – This rationale creates an intelligible differentia between financial debts and operational debts, which are unsecured, which is directly related to the object sought to be achieved by the Code – So long as there is some legitimate interest sought to be protected, having relation to the object sought to be achieved by the statute, Art. 14 does not get infracted – Constitution of India – Art. 14.

Object and reasons for the Code – Explained.

Enactment and working of the Code – Explained.

Companies Act, 2013: s. 412 – Selection of members of tribunal and appellate tribunal – Plea that appointment of members of the NCLT and the NCLAT contrary to Madras Bar Association (III)'s case – s. 412 whereby members of the tribunal and appellate tribunal to be selected, two judicial members of the Selection Committee get outweighed by three bureaucrats – Held: s. 412 has been amended by the Companies Amendment Act, 2017 – Present members of NCLT and NCLAT have been appointed by the Selection Committee, reconstituted in compliance with the direction of this Court.

Judiciary: NCLAT Bench – Creation of Circuit Benches –

Submission that NCLAT Bench has a seat only at New Delhi and is contrary to the judgment in Madras Bar Association (II) case –

Held: In view of the assurance by the Attorney General that Circuit Benches would be established soon, issuance of direction to Union of India to set up Circuit Benches of the NCLAT within the stipulated period. Constitution of India: Art. 77 – Submission that the tribunals NCLT and NCLAT are functioning under the wrong Ministry-Ministry of Corporate Affairs, however, as per the Madras Bar Association(I) case the administrative support for all the tribunals should be from the Ministry of Law and Justice – Held: Rules of business being mandatory in nature and having to be followed, are to be followed by the executive branch of the Government – However, this Court is being bound by the Madras Bar Association(I), the Union of India to follow the judgment, both in letter and spirit.

• • •

CHAPTER LIII

SSANGYONG ENGINEERING & CONSTRUCTION CO. LTD. Vs. NATIONAL HIGHWAYS AUTHORITY OF INDIA (NHAI), MAY 08, 2019

Citations: [2019] 7 SCR 522, 019(15) SCC 131

[R. F. NARIMAN AND VINEET SARAN, JJ.]

Arbitration and Conciliation Act, 1996 – ss.34(2)(b)(ii),

34(2)(a)(iii) – Respondent invited bids for construction of a four-lane bypass on National Highway 26 in the State of Madhya Pradesh

– Appellant's bid was accepted – Price adjustment for four of the components used in execution of the contract i.e. cement, steel, plant and machinery, and other local materials was to be calculated as per formula given in sub-clause 70.3 of the contract – Price adjustment was being paid to the appellant by using the Wholesale Price Index (WPI) published by the Ministry of Industrial Development, which followed the years 1993-94= 100 (Old Series) – However, w.e.f 14.09.10, the Ministry stopped publishing the WPI for the Old Series and started publishing indices under the WPI series 2004-05= 100 (New Series) – As both the indices C1 and Co were available to the appellant under the New Series for calculating price adjustment, the appellant raised bills accordingly – On 15.02.13, the respondent issued a Policy Circular in which a new formula for determining indices was used stating that the Circular would be applied to the contract in question, as a result of which, a linking factor would have to be provided by which the Old Series was connected to the New Series – Appellant challenged the Circular – Eventually, the arbitral tribunal consisting of three members by majority award held that the Circular could be applied as it was within contractual stipulations – Petition u/s.34 filed by the appellant – Rejected by the High Court – Appellant inter alia pleaded that s.34(2)(b)(ii) was attracted as the award was in conflict with the public policy of India and that s.34(2)(a)(iii) would also be attracted as principles of natural justice were violated – Held: Government guidelines that were referred to and relied upon by the majority award to arrive at the linking factor were never in evidence before the Tribunal – Tribunal relied upon the said guidelines by itself stating that they are to be found on a certain website – This being the case, the appellant would be directly affected, not being allowed to comment on the applicability or interpretation of those guidelines – Thus, majority award set aside u/s.34(2)(a)(iii) – Further, in order to apply a linking factor, a Circular, unilaterally issued by one party, cannot possibly bind the other party to the agreement without that other party's consent – Indeed, the Circular expressly stipulated that it cannot apply unless the contractors furnish an undertaking/ affidavit that the price adjustment under the Circular is acceptable to them – Appellant gave such undertaking only conditionally and without prejudice to its argument that the Circular does not and cannot apply – Majority award created a new contract for the parties by applying the said unilateral Circular and by substituting a workable formula under the agreement by another formula de hors the agreement – Thus, a fundamental principle of justice was breached – Such a course of conduct would be contrary to fundamental principles of justice as followed in this country and shocks the conscience of the Court – However, this ground is available only in very exceptional circumstances, as in the present case – Judgments of the Single Judge and the Division Bench of the High Court, set aside – Consequently, the majority award is also set aside – In order to do complete justice between the parties, invoking power u/Art.142 of the Constitution of India, the minority award is upheld – This award, together with interest now be executed between the parties – Foreign Awards (Recognition and Enforcement) Act, 1961 – s.7 – Constitution of India – Art.142 –

UNCITRAL Model Law on International Commercial Arbitration – Art.26.

Arbitration and Conciliation Act, 1996 – s.34 – Setting aside an arbitral award, in conflict with "public policy of India"– Law post Amendment Act, 2015 – Held: "Public policy of India", whether contained in s.34 or s.48 of the 1996 Act would now mean the "fundamental policy of Indian law" as explained in paragraphs 18 and 27 of Associate Builders case i.e. the fundamental policy of Indian law would be relegated to the "Renusagar" understanding of this expression – Expansion of the phrase "public policy of India", made in Western Geco case has been done away with –

Western Geco as explained in paragraphs 28 and 29 of Associate Builders, would no longer obtain, as under the guise of interfering with an award on the ground that the arbitrator has not adopted a judicial approach, the Court's intervention would be on the merits of the award, which cannot be permitted post amendment – However, principles of natural justice, as contained in ss.18 and 34(2)(a)(iii) of the 1996 Act continue to be grounds of challenge of an award, as is contained in paragraph 30 of Associate Builders – Arbitration and Conciliation (Amendment) Act, 2015.

Arbitration and Conciliation (Amendment) Act, 2015 –

Applicability of – Held: Section 34, as amended, will apply only to s.34 applications that have been made to the Court on or after 23.10.2015, irrespective of the fact that the arbitration proceedings may have commenced prior to that date – Arbitration and Conciliation Act, 1996 – s.34.

Interpretation of Statutes – Amendment by way of clarification – Retrospective or prospective – Held: Amendment made in Explanations 1 and 2 to s.34(2)(b)(ii) have been made for the avoidance of any doubt – Even on principle, it is the substance of the amendment that is to be looked at rather than the form –

Therefore, even in cases where, for avoidance of doubt, something is clarified by way of an amendment, such clarification cannot be retrospective if the earlier law has been changed substantively – Arbitration and Conciliation Act, 1996 – Explanations 1 and 2 to s.34(2)(b)(ii). Words & expressions – "Public policy of India" – Meaning of – Held: Public policy of India is now constricted to mean firstly, that a domestic award is contrary to the fundamental policy of Indian law, as understood in paragraphs 18 and 27 of Associate Builders case, or secondly, that such award is against basic notions of justice or morality as understood in paragraphs 36 to 39 of Associate Builders – Explanation 2 to s.34(2)(b)(ii) and Explanation 2 to s.48(2)(b)(ii) was added by the Amendment Act only so that Western Geco case, as understood in Associate Builders, and paragraphs 28 and 29 in particular, is now done away with – Arbitration and

Conciliation Act, 1996 – Explanation 2 to s.34(2)(b)(ii) & Explanation 2 to s.48(2)(b)(ii) – Arbitration and Conciliation (Amendment) Act, 2015.

Arbitration and Conciliation Act, 1996 – s.34(2A) –"Patent illegality" – Held: Insofar as domestic awards made in India are concerned, an additional ground is now available u/sub-s.(2A), added to s.34 by the Amendment Act, 2015– There must be patent illegality appearing on the face of the award, which refers to such illegality as goes to the root of the matter but which does not amount to mere erroneous application of the law – If an arbitrator is alleged to have wandered outside the contract and dealt with matters not allotted to him, this would be a jurisdictional error which could be corrected on the ground of "patent illegality", which would not apply to international commercial arbitrations that are decided under Part II of the 1996 Act – A decision which is perverse, as understood in paragraphs 31 and 32 of Associate Builders, while no longer being a ground for challenge under "public policy of India", would certainly amount to a patent illegality appearing on the face of the award – Arbitration and Conciliation (Amendment) Act, 2015.

Arbitration and Conciliation Act, 1996 – ss.28(3), 34(2A) –

Held: Change made in s.28(3) by the Amendment Act really follows what is stated in paragraphs 42.3 to 45 in Associate Builders case, namely, that the construction of the terms of a contract is primarily for an arbitrator to decide, unless the arbitrator construes the contract in a manner that no fair-minded or reasonable person would; that the arbitrator's view is not even a possible view to take – Also, if the arbitrator wanders outside the contract and deals with matters not allotted to him, he commits an error of jurisdiction – This ground of challenge will now fall within the new ground added u/s.34(2A) – Arbitration and Conciliation (Amendment) Act, 2015.

Arbitration and Conciliation Act, 1996 – s.34(2)(a)(iii) and ss.18, 24(3), 26 – Held: ss.18, 24(3) and 26 are important pointers to what is contained in the ground of challenge mentioned in s.34(2)(a)(iii) – Under s.34(2)(a)(iii), one of the grounds of challenge of an arbitral award is that a party is unable to present its case – Where materials are taken behind the back of the parties by the Tribunal, on which the parties have had no opportunity to comment, the ground u/s.34(2)(a)(iii) would be made out.

Arbitration and Conciliation Act, 1996 – s.34(2)(a)(iv) –

" submission to arbitration"– Challenge to an arbitral award – Held:

Where an arbitral tribunal has rendered an award which decides matters either beyond the scope of the arbitration agreement or beyond the disputes referred to the arbitral tribunal, the arbitral award could be said to have dealt with decisions on matters beyond the scope of submission to arbitration – To bring in by the backdoor grounds relatable to s.28(3) of the 1996 Act to be matters beyond the scope of submission to arbitration u/s.34(2)(a)(iv) would not be permissible as this ground must be construed narrowly and so construed, must refer only to matters which are beyond the arbitration agreement or beyond the reference to the arbitral tribunal.

Words & expressions –" most basic notions of ... justice"–

Meaning of – Held: Expression "most basic notions of ... justice" finds mention in Explanation 1 to sub-clause (iii) to s.34(2)(b) – Here, what is referred to is, substantively or procedurally, some fundamental principle of justice which has been breached, and which shocks the conscience of the Court – Arbitration and Conciliation Act, 1996 – Explanation 1 to sub-clause (iii) to s.34(2)(b).

• • •

CHAPTER LIV

DR. ASHWANI KUMAR Vs. UNION OF INDIA AND ANOTHER, SEPTEMBER 05, 2019

Citations: [2019] 12 SCR 30, 2019 SCC Online SC 1144

[RANJAN GOGOI, CJI, DINESH MAHESHWARI AND SANJIV KHANNA, JJ.]

Custodial Torture: Writ petition filed under Art.32 of the Constitution – Seeking effective and purposive legislative framework/law based upon the 'Convention against torture and Other Cruel, inhuman or Degrading Treatment or Punishment' adopted by the United Nations General Assembly – Prayer of applicant was that custodial torture being crime against humanity which directly infracts and violates Art.21, this court should invoke and exercise jurisdiction under Arts.141, 142 for protection and advancement of human dignity, a core and non-negotiable constitutional right – Held: It is true that in some extraordinary cases where notwithstanding the institutional reasons and the division of power, this Court has laid down general rules/guidelines when there has been a clear, substantive and gross human rights violation, which significantly outweighed and dwarfed any legitimising concerns based upon separation of powers, lack of expertise and uncertainty of the consequences – However, a mere allegation of violation of human rights or a plea raising environmental concerns cannot be the 'bright-line' to hold that self-restraint must give way to judicial legislation – Where and when directions should be issued by Court are questions and issues involving constitutional dilemmas that mandate a larger debate and discussion – Such directions are to be issued with great care and circumspection and certainly not when the matter is already pending consideration and debate with the executive or Parliament – This is not a case which requires Court's intervention to give a suggestion for need to frame a law as the matter is already pending active consideration – Any direction at this stage would be interpreted as judicial participation in the enactment of law – When the matter is already pending consideration and is being examined for the purpose of legislation, it would not be appropriate for this Court to enforce its opinion, be it in the form of a direction or even a request, for it would clearly undermine and conflict with the role assigned to the judiciary under the Constitution – No directions can be given to the executive to ratify the UN Convention for it would virtually amount to issuing directions to enact laws in conformity with the UN Convention – Constitution of India – Arts.21, 32, 141, 142. Constitution of India: Separation of powers – India has a written Constitution which is supreme and adumbrates as well as divides powers, roles and functions of the three wings of the State - the legislature, the executive and the judiciary – These divisions are boundaries and limits fixed by the Constitution to check and prevent transgression by any one of the three branches into the powers, functions and tasks that fall within the domain of the other wing – The three branches have to respect the constitutional division and not disturb the allocation of roles and functions between the triad – Adherence to the constitutional scheme dividing the powers and the rule of law is secured when each branch observes the constitutional limitations to their powers, functions and roles – Modern theory of separation of powers does not accept that the three branches perform mutually isolated roles and functions and accepts a need for coordinated institutional effort for good governance, albeit emphasise on benefits of division of power and labour by accepting the three wings do have separate and distinct roles and functions that are defined by the Constitution – All the institutions must act within their own jurisdictions and not trespass into the jurisdiction of other – By segregating the powers and functions of the institutions, the Constitution ensures a structure where the institutions function as per their institutional strengths.

Constitution of India: Powers and functions of legislature –

Held: The legislature as an elected and representative body enacts laws to give effect to and fulfil democratic aspirations of the people – Legislature functions as a deliberative and representative body – It is directly accountable and answerable to the electorate and citizens of this country – This representativeness and principle of accountability is what gives legitimacy to the legislations and laws made by Parliament or the state legislatures. Constitution of India: Arts.73 and 162 – Powers and functions of executive – Held: The executive has the primary responsibility of formulating government policies and proposing legislations which when passed by the legislature become laws – By virtue of Arts.73 and 162 of the Constitution, the powers and functions of the executive are wide and expansive, as they cover matters in respect of which Parliament/state legislature can make laws and vests with the executive the authority and jurisdiction exercisable by the Government of India or the State

Government, as the case may be –As a delegate of the legislative bodies and subject to the terms of the legislation, the executive makes second stage laws known as 'subordinate or delegated legislation' – In fields where there is no legislation, the executive has the power to frame policies, schemes, etc., which is co-extensive with the power of Parliament or the state legislature to make laws – At the same time, the political executive is accountable to the legislature and holds office till they enjoy the support and confidence of the legislature – Thus, there is interdependence, interaction and even commonality of personnel/ members of the legislature and the executive – The executive, therefore, performs multi-functional role and is not monolithic. Constitution of India: Role of judiciary – Judges unlike members of the legislature represent no one, strictly speaking not even the citizens – Judges are not accountable and answerable as the political executive is to the legislature and the elected representatives are to the electorate – This independence ensures that the judges perform the constitutional function of safeguarding the supremacy of the Constitution while exercising the power of judicial review in a fair and even-handed manner without pressure and favours – As an interpreter, guardian and protector of the Constitution, the judiciary checks and curbs violation of the Constitution by the Government when they overstep their constitutional limits, violate the basic structure of the Constitution, infringe fundamental rights or act contrary to law – Power of judicial review has expanded taking within its ambit the concept of social and economic justice – Yet, while exercising this power of judicial review, the courts do not encroach upon the field marked by the Constitution for the legislature and the executive, as the courts examine legality and validity of the legislation or the governmental action, and not the wisdom behind the legislative measure or relative merits or demerits of the governmental action – Neither does the Constitution permit the courts to direct, advise or sermonise others in the spheres reserved for them by the Constitution, provided the legislature or the executive do not transgress their constitutional limits or statutory conditions.

Doctrines/Principles: Doctrine of separation of power – The doctrine restrains the legislature from declaring the judgment of a court to be void and of no effect, while the legislature still possesses the legislative competence of enacting a validating law which remedies the defect pointed out in the judgment – However, this does not ordain and permit the legislature to declare a judgment as invalid by enacting a law, but permits the legislature to take away the basis of the judgment by fundamentally altering the basis on which it was pronounced – Therefore, while exercising all important checks and balances function, each wing should be conscious of the enormous responsibility that rests on them to ensure that institutional respect and comity is maintained – Constitution of India – Judgment/Order – Legislation. Doctrines/Principles: Doctrine of separation of power –

Distinction between interpretation and adjudication by the courts on one hand and the power to enact legislation by the legislature on the other – Adjudication results in what is often described as judge made law, but the interpretation of the statutes and the rights in accordance with the provisions of Articles 14, 19 and 21 in the course of adjudication is not an attempt or an act of legislation by the judges – Legislature itself entrusts the judiciary to lay down parameters in the form of precedents which is oft-spoken as judge made law – Such law, even if made by the judiciary, would not infringe the doctrine of separation of powers and is in conformity with the constitutional functions – Thus, law-making within certain limits is a legitimate element of a judge's role, if not inevitable – A judge has to adjudicate and decide on the basis of legal provisions, which when indeterminate on a particular issue require elucidation and explanation – This requires a judge to interpret the provisions to decide the case and, in this process, he may take recourse and rely upon fundamental rights, including the right to life, but even then he does not legislate a law while interpreting such provisions – Such interpretation is called 'judge made law' but not legislation – Constitution of India – Judge made law.

• • •

CHAPTER LV

ROJER MATHEW Vs. SOUTH INDIAN BANK LTD. & ORS. NOVEMBER 13, 2019

Citation: (2020) 6 SCC 1

[RANJAN GOGOI, CJI, N. V. RAMANA, DR D. Y. CHANDRACHUD, DEEPAK GUPTA

AND SANJIV KHANNA, JJ.]

Tribunals – Finance Act, 2017 – Finance Act, 2017, a 'money bill' or not u/Art.110 – Validity of the Act, 2017 – Held: The majority in K.S. Puttaswamy (Aadhaar-5) pronounced the nature of the impugned enactment without first delineating the scope of Art.110(1) and principles for interpretation or the repercussions of such process – The majority dictum in K.S. Puttaswamy (Aadhaar-5) did not substantially discuss the effect of the word 'only' in Art.110(1) and offers little guidance on the repercussions of a finding when some of the provisions of an enactment passed as a 'Money Bill' do not conform to Art. 110 (1) (a) (b) – Without expressing a firm and final opinion, the analysis in K.S. Puttaswamy (Aadhaar-5) made its application difficult to the present case and raises a potential conflict between the judgments of Coordinate Benches – Being a Bench of equal strength as that in K.S. Puttaswamy (Aadhaar-5), the batch of matters directed to be referred to the Larger Bench. Tribunals – Finance Act, 2017 – S. 184 – Constitutionality of s. 184 on account of excessive delegations – Held s.184 does not suffer from excessive delegations of legislative functions as there are adequate principles to guide framing of delegated legislation, which would include the binding dictums of the Supreme Court – The objects of the parent enactments as well as the law laid down by the Supreme Court in R.K. Jain, L. Chandra Kumar, R. Gandhi, Madras Bar Association and Gujarat Urja Vikas undoubtedly bind the delegate and mandatorily requires the delegate u/s. 184 to act strictly in conformity with these decisions and the objects of delegated legislation stipulated in the statutes Tribunals – The Tribunal, Appellate Tribunal and other Authorities (Qualifications, Experience and other Conditions of Service of Members) Rules, 2017 – Conformity of the Rules with the judicial principles inherent in the Constitutional scheme as established by the Supreme Court – Held: The composition of the search-cum-Selection

Committees under the Rules amounts to excessive interference of the Executive in appointment of members and presiding offices of statutory Tribunals and it is detrimental to the independence of Judiciary – In addition to this, there has been a blatant dilution of judicial character in appointments whereby candidates without any judicial experience are prescribed to be eligible for adjudicatory posts such as that of the presiding Officer – Therefore, the Rules have an effect of dilution of the judicial character in adjudicatory positions – Further, earlier removal of members or presiding officer was done after an enquiry by the Supreme Court Judges and with necessary consultation with the Chief Justice of India, under the present Rules it is permissible for the Central Government to appoint an enquiry Committee for removal of any presiding officer or member on its own – The Members and Presiding Officers of Tribunals cannot be removed without either the concurrence of the Judiciary or in the manner specified in the Constitution for Constitutional Court Judges – Also, there must be uniform age of superannuation for all members in all the Tribunals, the Rules demonstrate disparity in age of superannuation of

Members and Chairpersons/Presiding Officers of different Tribunals – Furthermore, there is inconsistency within the Rules with regard to the tenure prescribed for the Members of Tribunals insofar as a fixed tenure of three years for both direct appointments from the Bar and appointment of retired judicial officers or judges of High Court or Supreme Court – It is also discriminatory to the extent that it attempts to create equality between unequal classes – Therefore, the Rules suffer from various infirmities and are contrary to the Parent enactment and the principles envisaged in the Constitution, resultantly, directed to be struck down in entirety.

Tribunals – Finance Act, 2017 – Whether there should be a single Nodal Agency for administration of all Tribunals – Held: It may not be very crucial as to which Ministry or Department performs the duties of Nodal Agency for a Tribunal, but what is of utmost importance is that the Tribunal should not be expected to look towards such Nodal Agency for its day to day requirements – There must be a direction to allocate adequate and sufficient funds for each Tribunal to make it self-sufficient and selfsustainable authority for all intents and purposes.

Tribunals – A Judicial Impact Assessment of all tribunals in India – Need for – Held: It was directed in Salem Advocate Bar Association (II) v. Union of India for a Committee to be constituted to assess the need for Judicial Impact Assessment – Pursuant thereto, Jagannadha Rao Committee Report was submitted, it suggested that legislature must analyse the budgetary requirement of the staff, additional expenditure arising out of the new cases consequent to the enactment, the number of Civil and Criminal Cases expected to arise from the new enactment, the requirement of Judges etc. – The legislature has not conformed to the opinion of the Supreme Court with respect to 'Judicial Impact Assessment' and thus, has not made any attempt to assess the ramifications of the Finance Act, 2017 – Therefore, the Union of India directed to carry out Financial Impact Assessment in respect of all the Tribunals referable to ss. 158 to 182 of the Finance Act, 2017 and undertake an exercise to assess the need based requirements and make available sufficient resources for each Tribunal established by the Parliament. Tribunals – Judges of Tribunals set up by Acts of Parliament under Arts. 323-A and 323-B of the Constitution equated in 'Rank' and 'Status' with constitutional functionaries – Held: There can be no doubt that executive action cannot confer status equivalent to that either Supreme Court or High Court Judges on any member or head of any Tribunal or other judicial fora – Tribunals are not substitutes of Superior Courts and are only supplemental to them – Hence, the status of members of such Tribunals cannot be equated with that of the sitting Judges of Constitutional Courts. Tribunals – Direct Statutory appeals from Tribunals to the Supreme Court – Consideration of – Held: Such statutory appeals take away the inherent ability of the Supreme Court, as envisaged in the Constitution, to regulate cases before it by confining its consideration to cases involving the most egregious of wrongs and/ or having the greatest impact on public interest – It is evident that Supreme Court has lost its original character owing to the routine hearing of appeals through invocation of the discretionary jurisdiction u/Art. 136 – For the discharge of constitutional functions of deliberating on substantial questions of law, answering constitutional questions and resolving other issues of great Public importance, it is essential that Supreme Court has adequate time to apply its mind and consider matters in depth the practice of bringing every second case before the Supreme Court u/Art. 136 must be deprecated – Therefore, the Union of India in consultation with either the Law Commission or any other expert body revisit such provisions under various enactments providing for direct appeals to the Supreme Court against orders of Tribunals, and instead provide appeals to Division Benches of the High Courts, if at all necessary. Tribunals – Amalgamation of Existing Tribunals and setting up of Benches – Need for – Held: The 'importance' in distribution of case-load and inconsistencies in nature, location and functioning of Tribunals require urgent attention – It is essential that after conducting a Judicial Impact Assessment, Tribunals be amalgamed with others dealing with similar areas of law, to ensure effective utilisation of resources and to facilitate access to justice.

– Therefore, the Union Government directed to carry out an appropriate exercise for amalgamation of existing Tribunals adopting the test of homogeneity of the subject matters to be dealt with and thereafter constitute adequate number of Benches Commensurate with the existing and anticipated volume of work.

Tribunals – Tribunalisation – A global trend – Discussed.

• • •

CHAPTER LVI

CENTRAL PUBLIC INFORMATION OFFICER, SUPREME COURT OF INDIA Vs. SUBHASH CHANDRA AGARWAL, NOVEMBER 13, 2019

Citation: (2020) 5 SCC 481

[RANJAN GOGOI, CJI, N.V. RAMANA, DR. DHANANJAYA Y. CHANDRACHUD, DEEPAK GUPTA

AND SANJIV KHANNA, JJ.]

Right to Information Act, 2005 – Collegium system for appointment and elevation of judges to the Supreme Court and the High Courts; declaration of assets by judges, etc. – Information in context of – The respondent filed three applications under the RTI Act, 2005 seeking information regarding: 1) copies of the correspondence exchanged between constitutional authorities together with file noting, relating to the appointment of three Judges of the Supreme Court, who had superseded seniority of another three Judges by an application dated 23.01.2009; 2) a copy of the resolution dated 07.05.1997 of the Judges of the Supreme Court requiring every sitting Judge and all the future judges upon assuming office to make a declaration of assets by an application dated 10.11.2007 and 3) on the basis of a newspaper report, the complete correspondence exchanged with the Chief Justice of India in regards to a Union Minister having allegedly approached a judge of the High court, through a lawyer to influence a judicial decision by an application dated 06.07.2009.

– In an application dated 06.07.2009, the information was denied by the CPIO of the Supreme Court on the ground that the information sought by the respondent was not handled and dealt with by the Registry of the Supreme Court and neither maintained nor available with Registry – However, the Central Information Commission (CIC) directed disclosure of information and observed that disclosure will not infringe upon the status of the Judges – The information sought in application 23.01.2009 was again denied by CPIO observing that the Supreme Court Registry did not deal with the matters pertaining to appointment of the Judges of the Supreme Court – However, the CIC directed the furnishing of information – Insofar as application dated 10.11.2007 is concerned, it was also dismissed by the CPIO and the CIC again directed the CPIO of the Supreme Court to provide the information asked by the respondent in his RTI application unless, the disclosure of information was exempted by law – The appellant instituted writ petition before the Delhi High Court and the same was dismissed holding, inter alia, that the declaration of assets furnished by the Judges of the Supreme Court to Chief Justice of India and its contents constituted 'information', subject to the provisions of the RTI Act – The Full Bench of the High Court upheld the decision of the Single Judge of the High Court – Aggrieved by the decision of the Full Bench of the High Court and the CIC in the RTI applications, the CPIO, Supreme Court has preferred the appeals before the Supreme Court against the order of the CIC in applications dated 06.07.2009, 23.01.2009 and the decision of the Full Bench of the High Court – Held [Per Sanjiv Khanna, J. (for himself, Ranjan Gogoi, CJI, and N.V. Ramana, Dr. D.Y. Chandrachud and Deepak Gupta, JJ.)]: The information sought by the respondent in application dated 10.11.2007, regarding declaration of the assets, the judgment of the Full Bench of the High Court is upheld, which had upheld the order passed by the CIC directing the CPIO, Supreme Court to furnish information on the Judges of the Supreme Court who had declared their assets –

Such disclosure would not in any way, impinge upon the personal information and right to privacy of the judges – The fiduciary relationship rule in terms of cl(e) to s. 8(1) of the RTI Act is inapplicable – It would not affect the right to confidentiality of the Judges and their right to protect personal information and privacy, which would be the case where the details and contents of personal assets in the declaration are called for and sought in which event the public interest test as applicable vide s. 8(1)(j) and proviso to s.11(1) of the RTI Act would come into operation – As far as other two RTI applications dated 06.07.2009 and 23.01.2009 are concerned, these application are remitted to the CPIO, Supreme Court to re-examine the matter after following the procedure u/s. 11(1) of the RTI Act as information relates to third parties. Right to Information Act, 2005 – s.2 cl(h) and sub-cl (ii) in cl(e) to s.2 – Whether the Supreme Court of India and the Chief Justice of India are two separate public Authorities – Held [Per Sanjiv Khanna, J. (for himself, Ranjan Gogoi, CJI, and N.V. Ramana, Dr. D.Y. Chandrachud and Deepak Gupta, JJ.)] : It is undebatable that the Supreme Court is a 'public authority', as defined vide cl(h) to s.2 of the RTI Act as it has been established and constituted by or under the Constitution of India – The office of the Chief Justice or for that matter the judges is not separate from the Supreme Court and is part and parcel of the Supreme Court as a body, authority and institution – The Chief Justice and the Supreme Court are not two distinct and separate 'public authorities', albeit, the latter is a 'public authority' and the Chief Justice and the Judges together form and constitute the 'public authority', that is, the Supreme Court of India.

Right to Information Act, 2005 – s.2 cl.(f)(i) and (j) –

Information and Right to Information – Held [Per Sanjiv Khanna, J. (for himself, Ranjan Gogoi, CJI, and N.V. Ramana, Dr. D.Y. Chandrachud and Deepak Gupta, JJ.)] : What is explicit as well as implicit from the definition of 'information' in cl.(f) to s. 2 follows and gets affirmation from the definition of 'right to information' that the information should be accessible by the public authority and 'held by or under the control of any public authority' – The words 'under the control of any public authority' as per their natural meaning would mean the right and power of the public authority to get access to the information – It refers to dominion over the information or the right to any material, document etc. –

The words 'under the control of any public authority' would include within their ambit and scope information relating to a private body which can be accessed by a public authority under any other law for the time being in force subject to the pre-imposed conditions and restrictions as applicable to access the information. Right to Information Act, 2005 – s. 8(1)(e) – Relationship between the Chief Justice and Judges – Held [Per Sanjiv Khanna, J. (for himself, Ranjan Gogoi, CJI, and N.V. Ramana, Dr. D.Y. Chandrachud and Deepak Gupta, JJ.)] : Ordinarily the relationship between the Chief Justice and Judges would not be that of fiduciary and a beneficiary – However, it is not an absolute rule/code for in certain situation and acts, fiduciary relationship may arise – Whether or not such a relationship arises in a particular situation would have to be dealt with on the tests and parameters. Right to Information Act, 2005 – Fiduciary relationship u/s. 8(1)(e) – The appellant argued that the information about the assets of judges is exempt from disclosure, by virtue of s. 8(1)(e) – Held [Per Dr. D.Y. Chandrachud, J.]: The Chief Justice of India merely holds the information in accordance with the official functions and not in any fiduciary capacity – The judges who disclose their assets cannot be said to be vulnerable to and dependent on the Chief Justice of India – In these circumstances, it cannot be held that asset information shared with the Chief Justice of India, by the Judges of the Supreme Court, are held by him in a fiduciary capacity, which, if revealed, would result in breach of fiduciary duty.

Right to Information Act, 2005 – s.8(1)(j) and s.11 – Held:

[Per Dr. D.Y. Chandrachud, J.]: ss.8 and 11 must be read together – In every case where the information requested is "personal information" within the operation of cl.(j) of sub-section 1 of s.8, the procedure of notice and objections u/s.11 must be complied with – The two provisions create a substantive systems of checks and balances which seek to balance the right of the information applicant to receive information with the third party to prevent the disclosure of personal information by permitting the letter to contest the proposed disclosure. Right to Information Act, 2005 – Public Interest – Held [Per Sanjiv Khanna, J. (for himself, Ranjan Gogoi, CJI, and N.V. Ramana, Dr. D.Y. Chandrachud and Deepak Gupta, JJ.)] : The Public interest test in the context of the RTI Act would mean reflecting upon the object and purpose behind the right to information, the right to privacy and consequences of invasion, and breach of confidentiality and possible harm and injury that would be caused to the third party, with reference to a particular information and the person.

Right to Information Act, 2005 – Judicial Independence –

Held : [Per Sanjiv Khanna, J. (for himself, Ranjan Gogoi, CJI, and N.V. Ramana, Dr. D.Y. Chandrachud and Deepak Gupta, JJ.)]:

The independence of the judiciary is a matter of ennobled public concern and directly relates to public welfare and would be one of the factors to be taken into account in weighing and applying the public interest test – Thus, when the public interest demand the disclosure of information, judicial independence has to be kept in mind while deciding the question of exercise of discretion –

Reference to the principle of judicial independence is not to undermine and avoid accountability which is an aspect to be taken into account while examining the public interest in favour of disclosure of information. Right to Information Act, 2005 – Transparency, judicial independence and RTI Act – Held [Per N.V. Ramana, J.]: There needs to be balance between the three equally important concepts

– As a shield, the judicial independence is the basis with which Judiciary has maintained its trust reposed by the citizens – The judiciary needs to be protected from attempts to breach its independence – Such interference requires calibration of appropriate amount of transparency in consonance with judicial independence – The right to information should not be allowed to be used as a tool of surveillance to scuttle effective functioning of judiciary.

Right to Information Act, 2005 – s.8 – non-exhaustive considerations while assessing the 'public interest'– Held [Per N.V. Ramana, J.]: The following non- exhaustive considerations needs to be considered while assessing the 'public interest' under Section 8 of the RTI Act- a) Nature and content of the information; b) Consequences of non-disclosure; dangers and benefits to public; c) Type of confidential obligation; d) Beliefs of the confidant; reasonable suspicion; e) Party to whom information is disclosed; f) Manner in which information acquired; g)Public and private interests; h) Freedom of expression and proportionality.

• • •

CHAPTER LVII

COMMITTEE OF CREDITORS OF ESSAR STEEL INDIA LIMITED THROUGH AUTHORISED SIGNATORY Vs. SATISH KUMAR GUPTA & ORS. NOVEMBER 15, 2019

Citation: (2020) 8 SCC 531

[R. F. NARIMAN, SURYA KANT AND V. RAMASUBSRAMANIAN, JJ.]

Insolvency and Bankruptcy Code, 2016 – Corporate Insolvency Resolution Process – Power of Committee of creditors to approve resolution plan - On facts, resolution plans for Corporate debtor-Essar Steel India Limited – In CIRP of corporate debtor, ArcelorMittal India was successful resolution applicant – Resolution plan of ArcelorMittal specifically providing for an upfront payment of INR 35,000 crores in order to resolve debts amounting to INR 42,213 crores – Approval of final resolution plan of Arcelor Mittal by Committee of Creditors – Initiation of several proceedings – NCLT allowed the resolution plan – Challenge to, before NCLAT – NCLAT held that there can be no difference between a financial creditor and operational creditor in the matter of payment of dues; thus, NCLAT re-distributed the proceeds payable under the approved resolution plan as per the method of calculation adopted by it so that all financial creditors and operational creditors be paid 60.7% of their admitted claims;

NCLAT directed that each financial creditor (whether secured or unsecured) with a claim equal to or more than INR 10 lakhs be paid 60.7% of its admitted claim irrespective of their security interest; that operational creditors with a claim of equal to or more than INR 1 crore be paid 60.268% of their admitted claims; that Committee of Creditors not empowered to decide the manner of distribution to be made between one or other creditors; that s. 53 cannot be applied during the corporate resolution process but will apply only at the stage of liquidation; and that the claims decided by the resolution professional and affirmed by the Adjudicating Authority or the Appellate Tribunal are final and binding on all creditors – On appeal, held: Order by NCLAT which substitutes its wisdom for the commercial wisdom of the Committee of Creditors and also directs the admission of a number of claims which was done by the resolution applicant, is set aside - CIRP of the corporate debtor will take place in accordance with the resolution plan of ArcelorMittal dated 23.10.2018, as amended and accepted by the Committee of Creditors on 27.03.2019, as it has provided for amounts to be paid to different classes of creditors by following s. 30(2) and Regulation 38 of the Code.

Insolvency and Bankruptcy Code, 2016 – Resolution professional – Role of, in the revival of the corporate debtor –

Held: Role of resolution professional is not adjudicatory but administrative - Resolution professional manages the affairs of the corporate debtor as a going concern from the stage of admission of an application u/ss. 7, 9 or 10 - He appoints and convenes meetings of the Committee of Creditors – He collects, collates and finally admit claims of all creditors, which must then be examined for payment, by the resolution applicant and be finally negotiated and decided by the Committee of Creditors. Prospective resolution applicant - Role of – Explained. Insolvency and Bankruptcy Code, 2016 – Committee of creditors - Role of, in the corporate resolution process – Held: Committee of Creditors decides on whether or not to rehabilitate the corporate debtor by means of acceptance of a particular resolution plan – Committee of Creditors may approve a resolution plan by a vote of not less than 66% of the voting share of the financial creditors, after considering its feasibility and viability, and various other requirements as may be prescribed by the Regulations - Ultimately it is the commercial wisdom of the Committee of Creditors which operates to approve the best resolution plan, which is finally accepted after negotiation of its terms by such Committee with prospective resolution applicants – Furthermore, the Committee of Creditors does not act in any fiduciary capacity to any group of creditors, on the contrary, it is to take a business decision based upon ground realities by a majority, which then binds all stakeholders, including dissentient creditors - Thus, commercial wisdom of this majority of creditors is important which is to determine, through negotiation with the prospective resolution applicant, as to how and in what manner the corporate resolution process is to take place –ss. 21, 24, 28, 29, 30 and 31.Insolvency and Bankruptcy Code, 2016 – National Company Law Tribunal- Adjudicating Authority and National Company Law Appellate Tribunal-Appellate Tribunal under – Jurisdiction of, qua resolution approved by Committee of Creditors – Held: Adjudicating Authority's jurisdiction is circumscribed by s. 30(2) and Appellate Tribunal's jurisdiction is circumscribed by s. 32 rw s. 61(3) -

Adjudicating Authority cannot interfere on merits with the commercial decision taken by the Committee of Creditors, the limited judicial review available is to see that the Committee of Creditors has taken into account the fact that the corporate debtor needs to keep going as a going concern during the insolvency resolution process; that it needs to maximise the value of its assets; and that the interests of all stakeholders including operational creditors has been taken care of - If the Adjudicating Authority finds, on a given set of facts, that the said parameters have not been kept in view, it may send a resolution plan back to the Committee of Creditors to re-submit such plan after satisfying the said parameters - Reasons given by the Committee of Creditors while approving a resolution plan may be looked at by the Adjudicating Authority only from this point of view, and once it is satisfied that Committee of Creditors has paid attention to these key features, it must then pass the resolution plan, other things being equal.

Insolvency and Bankruptcy Code, 2016 – Secured and unsecured creditors – Equality principle – Held: Secured and unsecured financial creditors are differentiated when it comes to amounts to be paid under a resolution plan, together with what dissenting secured or unsecured financial creditors are to be paid - Operational creditors are separately viewed from these secured and unsecured financial creditors in S.No.5 of paragraph 7 of statutory Form H - Thus, it can be seen that the Code and the Regulations, read as a whole, lead to the conclusion that the equality principle cannot be stretched to treating unequal equally, as that will destroy the very objective of the Code to resolve stressed assets - Equitable treatment is to be accorded to each creditor depending upon the class to which it belongs: secured or unsecured, financial or operational. Insolvency and Bankruptcy Code, 2016 – s. 21(8), 28 - Constitution of a sub-committee by the Committee of Creditors – Permissibility of – Plea that the Committee of Creditors delegated its functions to a sub-committee, as a result of which, the subcommittee secretly made negotiations with ArcelorMittal – Held:

Section 28(1)(h) provides that though the powers of Committee of Creditors are administrative in nature, they shall not be delegated to any other person – Power of approval of resolution plan u/s. 30(4), also cannot be delegated to any other body - However, subcommittees can be appointed for the purpose of negotiating with resolution applicants, or for performing other ministerial or administrative acts, provided such acts are in the ultimate analysis approved and ratified by the Committee of Creditors – On facts, every single administrative decision qua approving and administering the resolution plan submitted by Arcelor Mittal was in fact done by the requisite majority of the Committee of Creditors itself, the sub-committee having been used only for purposes of initiating proceedings and negotiating with ArcelorMittal, which ultimately culminated in the resolution plan as finally negotiated, being passed by the requisite majority of creditors – Standard Chartered Bank voted in favour of the constitution of a subcommittee and also requested for inclusion of its name in sub committee, however, when the Standard Chartered Bank found that things were going against it that it started raising objections on the technical plea that sub-committees cannot be constituted under the Code, thus, plea was not bonafide and is rejected. Insolvency and Bankruptcy Code, 2016 – s. 31(1) -

Extinguishment of Personal Guarantees and Undecided Claims – Held: s. 31(1) makes it clear that once a resolution plan is approved by the Committee of Creditors it shall be binding on all stakeholders, including guarantors – It cannot be said that part of the resolution plan which states that the claims of the guarantor on account of subrogation shall be extinguished, cannot be applied to the guarantees furnished by the erstwhile directors of the corporate debtor – A successful resolution applicant cannot suddenly be faced with “undecided” claims after the resolution plan submitted by him has been accepted as this would lead to uncertainty regarding amounts payable by a prospective resolution applicant who successfully took over the business of the corporate debtor - All claims must be submitted to and decided by the resolution professional so that a prospective resolution applicant knows exactly what has to be paid in order that it may then take over and run the business of the corporate debtor – Successful resolution applicant does on a fresh slate. Insolvency and Bankruptcy Code (Amendment) Act, 2019 –

ss. 4 and 6 – Constitutional Validity of – Held: As regards s. 4 of the Amendment Act, it is clear that as per s. 12 of the principal Act, the Corporate Insolvency Resolution proceedings should be mandatorily completed within a period of 330 days including any extension and legal proceedings related to resolution process of corporate debtor – Further grace period of 90 days is given, failing which corporate debtor shall be sent into liquidation – While leaving the provision otherwise intact, the word “mandatorily” is struck down as being manifestly arbitrary under Article 14 of the Constitution and as being an excessive and unreasonable restriction on the litigant’s right to carry on business under Article 19(1)(g) of the

Constitution – As regards, the substitution of s. 30(2)(b) by s. 6 of the Amending Act of 2019, it is constitutionally valid since the substituted s. 30(2)(b) is in fact a beneficial provision in favour of operational creditors and dissentient financial creditors as they are now to be paid a certain minimum amount, the minimum in the case of operational creditors being the higher of the two figures calculated under sub-clauses (i) and (ii) of clause (b), and the minimum in the case of dissentient financial creditor being a minimum amount that was not earlier payable – Furthermore, Explanation 1 and 2 as also sub-clause (b) of s. 6 of the Amending Act of 2019, is constitutionally valid.

CHAPTER LVIII

M/S SHANTI CONDUCTORS (P) LTD. Vs. ASSAM STATE ELECTRICITY BOARD AND ORS. DECEMBER 18, 2019

Citation: (2020) 2 SCC 677

[ASHOK BHUSHAN, S. ABDUL NAZEER AND NAVIN SINHA, JJ.]

Code of Civil Procedure, 1908:

Order 47 r. 1 – Review petition – Error apparent on record – On facts, review petition on the ground that there is an apparent error in the judgment by this Court holding that suit was barred by time – Petitioner's case that in money suit pertaining to interest on principal amount received by the petitioner, the last supply was completed on 04.10.93 but the last payment was made on 05.03.1994, a fresh period of limitation would begin from 05.03.1994 on the basis of s. 19 of the Limitation Act – Held: Exemption provided u/ss. 4 to 20 of the Limitation Act, are based on certain facts and events – On facts, perusal of the plaint indicates that there is no pleading as to exception of limitation by running any fresh period of limitation as per s. 19 – There was no occasion for defendants to raise any reply in reference to s. 19 –

Also, proviso to Order 7 r. 6 cannot come to the rescue of the plaintiff since the plaintiffs specifically pleaded that the provisions of the Limitation Act are not applicable since Act, 1993 has overriding effect – Furthermore, in the paragraph of cause of action for the suit, the cause of action is not claimed from the date 05.03.1994, which was the date when the last payment was received by the petitioner – Petitioner in the plaint has clearly not pleaded for benefit of s. 19 nor has brought necessary facts to enable the Court to consider the claim under s. 19 – Thus, the petitioner is not entitled for benefit of s. 19 and there is no error in the judgment of this Court holding that the suit of the plaintiff was barred by time – Furthermore, benefit of s. 14 of Limitation Act cannot be claimed by the plaintiff since writ petition, which was filed by the Association was by different entity – Issue of benefit of s. 14 was specifically considered and rejected by this Court in its judgment thus, there is no error apparent on the said ground – Limitation Act, 1963 – ss. 19, 14 – Interest on Delayed Payment to Small

Scale and Ancillary Industrial Undertakings Act, 1993.

Order 47 r. 1 – Review petitions – Error apparent on record – On facts, matter pertaining to interest on delayed payment to small scale industries – Review petition on the ground that there was error on face of record in observation of this Court – Some of the supplies made prior to commencement of the 1993 Act– 23.09.1992 and some of the supplies made after 23.09.1992 – Entitlement of petitioner to the benefit of interest under the 1993 Act – Held: The date of bill for the payment for supply of the materials by the plaintiffs was 29.09.1992 – This Court in the judgment rightly held that there was nothing on record to come to the conclusion that any supply was made after the enforcement of the Act so as to enable the appellant to claim interest u/s. 3 read with s. 4 of the 1993 Act, thus, the judgment of the High Court does not call for interference – Submission that there is error apparent on the face of record is rejected and the review petition is dismissed – Interest on Delayed Payment to Small Scale and Ancillary Industrial Undertakings Act, 1993.

Order 47 r. 1 – Review petition – Error apparent on record – Review petition on the ground that this Court dismissed the appeal as not maintainable which is error apparent on record –

Held: This Court considered the maintainability of appeal and found against the petitioner, thus, there is no ground to review the petition.

Order 47 r. 1 – Review petition – Scope of – Held: Scope of review is limited – Under the guise of review, petitioner cannot be permitted to reagitate and reargue the questions, which have already been addressed and decided.

Order 7 r. 6 – Grounds of exemption from limitation law – Applicability of – Held: When suit is instituted after expiration of period prescribed by law of limitation, the plaint should show the ground upon which exemption from such law is claimed – However, the Court may permit the plaintiff to claim exemption from the law of limitation on any ground not set out in the plaint, if such ground is not inconsistent with the grounds set out in the plaint.

Limitation Act, 1963: s. 19 – Benefit of – Held: Section 19 provide for a fresh period of limitation – Benefit under s. 19 is available when payment on account of debt or of interest on legacy is made before the expiration of the prescribed period by the person liable to pay the debt or legacy and an acknowledgement of the payment appears in the handwriting of, or in a writing signed by, the person making the payment.

• • •

CHAPTER LIX

KEISHAM MEGHACHANDRA SINGH Vs. THE HON'BLE SPEAKER MANIPUR LEGISLATIVE ASSEMBLY & ORS. JANUARY 21, 2020

Citation: 2020 (2) SCALE 329

[R. F. NARIMAN, ANIRUDDHA BOSE AND V. RAMASUBRAMANIAN, JJ.]

Constitution of India – Tenth Schedule – Disqualification of a candidate nominated in Legislative Assembly elections on ground of defection – The election for the 11th Manipur Legislative Assembly was conducted in March, 2017 – None of the political parties were able to secure a majority i.e. 31 seats in a Legislative Assembly of 60 seats in order to form the Government – The Congress Party emerged as the single largest party with 28 seats and BJP with 21 seats – The respondent no. 3 contested as a candidate nominated and set up by the Congress party and was duly elected – On 12.03.2017, respondent no. 3 along with various BJP members met the Governor of the State and staked a claim for forming a BJP-led Government – Thereafter, the respondent no. 3 was sworn in as a Minister in BJP-led government – Applications were filed before the Speaker of the legislative Assembly between April and July, 2017 seeking disqualification of the respondent no. 3 under paragraph 2(1)(a) of the Tenth Schedule – No action was taken by the Speaker – Held: It is clear from a reading of the judgment in Rajendra Singh Rana and S.A. Sampath Kumar that a failure to exercise jurisdiction vested in a Speaker cannot be covered by the shield contained in paragraph 6 of the Tenth Schedule, and that when a Speaker refrains from deciding a petition within a reasonable time, there was clearly an error which attracted jurisdiction of the High court in exercise of the power of judicial review – Further, Kihoto Hollohan do not in any manner, interdict judicial review in aid of the Speaker arriving at a prompt decision as to disqualification under the provisions of the Tenth Schedule – The Speaker, in acting as a Tribunal under the Tenth Schedule is bound to decide disqualification petitions within a reasonable period – What is reasonable will depend on the facts of each case, but absent exceptional circumstances for which there is good reason, a period of three months from the date on which the petition is filed is the outer limit within which the disqualification petition filed before the Speaker must be decided if the Constitutional objective of disqualifying persons who have infracted the Tenth Schedule is to be adhered to – The only relief that can be given in these instant appeals is that the Speaker of the Legislative Assembly be directed to decide the disqualification petitions pending before him within a period of four weeks from the date on which this judgment is intimated to him.

Words and Phrases – "Quia timet" – Discussed.

• • •

CHAPTER LX

SUSHILA AGGARWAL AND OTHERS Vs. STATE (NCT OF DELHI) AND ANOTHER, JANUARY 29, 2020

Citation: (2020) 5 SCC 1

[ARUN MISHRA, INDIRA BANERJEE, VINEET SARAN, M. R. SHAH AND S. RAVINDRA BHAT, JJ.]

Code of Criminal Procedure, 1973 – ss.437, 438, 439 and 167(2) – Order u/s.438 granting anticipatory bail – Life and operation of – Conflicting views of different Benches of varying strength as to whether the protection granted u/s.438 should be limited to a fixed period so as to enable the person to surrender before Trial Court and seek regular bail; whether the life of an anticipatory bail should end at the time and stage when the accused is summoned by the court – Reference to larger Bench – Held: (Per Curiam) Protection granted u/s.438 should not invariably be limited to a fixed period; it should inure in favour of the accused without any restriction on time – Normal conditions u/s.437(3) r/w s.438(2) should be imposed; if there are specific facts or features in regard to any offence, it is open for the court to impose any appropriate condition (including fixed nature of relief, or its being tied to an event) etc. – Further, the life or duration of an anticipatory bail order does not end normally at the time and stage when the accused is summoned by the court, or when charges are framed, but can continue till the end of the trial – Again, if there are any special or peculiar features necessitating the court to limit the tenure of anticipatory bail, it is open for it to do so – Observations in Siddharam Satlingappa Mhetre case (and other similar judgments) that no restrictive conditions at all can be imposed, while granting anticipatory bail are overruled – Likewise, the decision in Salauddin Abdulsamad Shaikh case and subsequent decisions which lay down such restrictive conditions, or terms limiting the grant of anticipatory bail, to a period of time are overruled – Guiding principles enumerated for Courts to follow while dealing with applications of Criminal Procedure Amendment Act, 2018 – Penal Code, 1860 –ss.376(3), 376AB, 376DA, 376DB – Constitution of India – Art.21

– Evidence Act, 1872 – s.27 – Interpretation of Statutes.

Answering the referred questions, the Court

HELD: 1.1 PER M. R. SHAH, J.

The expression “anticipatory bail” has not been defined in the Code. As observed by Supreme Court in the case of Balchand Jain, “anticipatory bail” means “bail in anticipation of arrest”. As held, the expression “anticipatory bail” is a misnomer inasmuch as it is not as if bail is presently granted by the Court in anticipation of arrest. An application for “anticipatory bail” in anticipation of arrest could be moved by the accused at a stage before an FIR is filed or at a stage when FIR is registered but the charge sheet has not been filed and the investigation is in progress or at a stage after the investigation is concluded. Power to grant “anticipatory bail” under Section 438 of the Cr.P.C. vests only with the Court of Sessions or the High Court. Therefore, ultimately it is for the concerned court to consider the application for “anticipatory bail” and while granting the “anticipatory bail” it is ultimately for the concerned court to impose conditions including the limited period of “anticipatory bail”, depends upon the stages at which the application for anticipatory bail is moved. A person in whose favour a pre-arrest bail order is made under Section 438 of the Cr.P.C. has to be arrested. However, once there is an order of pre-arrest bail/anticipatory bail, as and when he is arrested he has to be released on bail. Otherwise, there is no distinction or difference between the pre-arrest bail order under Section 438 and the bail order under Section 437 & 439 of the Cr.P.C. The only difference between the pre-arrest bail order under Section 438 and the bail order under Sections 437 and 439 is the stages at which the bail order is passed. The bail order under Section 438 of the Cr.P.C. is prior to his arrest and in anticipation of his arrest and the order of bail under Sections 437 and 439 is after a person is arrested. A bare reading of Section 438 of the Cr.P.C. shows that there is nothing in the language of the Section which goes to show that the pre-arrest bail granted under Section 438 has to be time bound. The position is the same as in Section 437 and Section 439 of the Cr.P.C. [Para 7.1][33EH, 34A-D]

• • •

CHAPTER LXI

DHEERAJ MOR Vs. HON'BLE HIGH COURT OF DELHI, FEBRUARY 19, 2020

Citation: (2020) 7 SCC 401

[ARUN MISHRA, VINEET SARAN AND S. RAVINDRA BHAT, JJ.]

Constitution of India – Arts.233-235 – Interpretation of Art.233 – Eligibility of members of subordinate judicial service for appointment as District Judge against the quota reserved for bar members by way of direct recruitment – Petitioners who are in judicial service inter alia claimed that there are two sources of recruitment u/Art.233(2)- from judicial service and from the bar; thus, a person in judicial service with 7 years practice at the bar before joining service (or combined with service as a judicial officer), can compete with members of the bar (with 7 or more years' practice), for direct recruitment, in the quota earmarked to be filled by such advocates – Matter referred by Division Bench of Supreme Court – Answering the reference, Held: Per Arun Mishra and Vineet Saran, JJ. – Members in the judicial service of the State can be appointed as District Judges by way of promotion/limited competitive examination – For the purpose of Art.232(2), an advocate continuing in practice for not less than 7 years as on the cut-off date and at the time of appointment as District Judge can be appointed as District Judge by way of direct recruitment if he is not already in the judicial service of the Union or a State – Members of judicial service having 7 years' of practice before joining service (or combined with service as a judicial officer) are not eligible to apply for direct recruitment as a District Judge – Rules framed by High Court against the posts reserved for Advocates by way of direct recruitment, are not ultra vires and are in conformity with Arts.14, 16 & 233 – In cases where in-service incumbents were appointed by way of direct recruitment from bar (in view of various interim orders passed by Supreme Court in Dheeraj Mor and other cases, though later vacated), in view of dismissal of the writ petitions filed by judicial officers, they cannot continue as District Judges – To be reverted to their original post – In case their right in channel for promotion had already ripened, and their juniors were promoted, High Court to consider their promotion in accordance with prevailing rules – Per S. Ravindra Bhat, J. (Supplementing) – Under Art.233, a judicial officer, regardless of her or his previous experience as an Advocate with seven years' practice can not apply, and compete for appointment to any vacancy in the post of District Judge – Her/ his chance to occupy that post would be through promotion, in accordance with Rules framed u/Art.234 and proviso to Art.309 – Exclusion- by the rules, from consideration of judicial officers, to the post of District Judges, in the quota earmarked for advocates with the requisite standing, or practice, conforms to the mandate of Arts. 233-235, and the rules are valid – Service Law – Higher Judicial Service – Interpretation of Statutes.

Constitution of India – Arts. 233(1), 234, 235 – Held: Per Arun Mishra and Vineet Saran, JJ. – Governor of a State is the authority for the purpose of appointment, promotion, posting and transfer – Eligibility is governed by Rules framed u/Arts. 234 & 235 – Per S. Ravindra Bhat, J. (Supplementing) – Governor of a State has the authority to make "appointments of persons to be, and the posting and promotion of, district judges in any State – While so appointing, the Governor is bound to consult the High Court – Art. 233 (1) cannot be construed as a source of appointment; it merely delineates as to who is the appointing authority – In matters relating to initial posting, initial appointment, and promotion of District Judges, the Governor has the authority to issue the order; thereafter it is up to the High Court, by virtue of Art.235, to exercise control and superintendence over the conditions of service of such District Judges – Service Law – Higher Judicial Service.

Constitution of India – Art. 233(2) – Eligibility of judicial officers to compete as against the post of District Judge by way of direct recruitment – Participation in selection process vis-à-vis appointment – Plea of petitioners placing reliance on Vijay Kumar Mishra & Anr. v. High Court of Judicature at Patna & Ors. reported as [2016] 3 SCR 806 in which it was held that the bar prescribed u/Art.233(2) prohibits only the appointment of persons in service of Central/State Govt. and not their participation in the recruitment process and in case they are selected, they can resign and join the post – Held: Per Arun Mishra and Vineet Saran, JJ. – Vijay Kumar Mishra providing eligibility of judicial officer to compete as against the post of District Judge by way of direct recruitment, does not lay down the law correctly – Overruled – Per S. Ravindra Bhat, J. (Supplementing) – Vijay Kumar Mishra, as far as it makes a distinction between consideration of a candidate's eligibility at the stage of selection, and eligibility reckonable at the time of appointment, is incorrect – Eligibility of any candidate is to be reckoned not from the date of his or her selection, but in terms of the rules, or the advertisement for the post – Service Law – Higher Judicial Service.

Service Law – Higher Judicial Service – Recruitment to the posts of District Judges from two sources- in-service and from the Bar – Claim by candidates from judicial service as against the posts reserved for direct recruitment from the Bar – Held: Per Arun Mishra and Vineet Saran, JJ. – Makers of the Constitution visualised and the law administered in the country for last seven decades reveals that the aforesaid modes of recruitment and two separate sources are recognised – No room to entertain submission of discrimination based on Arts.14 & 16 – Art.233(2) starts with the negative "not," which disentitles the claim of judicial officers against the post reserved for practicing advocates/pleaders – Per S. Ravindra Bhat, J. (Supplementing) – Since the Constitution itself makes a distinction between advocates on the one hand, and judicial officers, on the other, the argument of discrimination is insubstantial – Constitution of India – Arts.14, 16 & 233.

Constitution of India – Arts. 124, 217, 233(2) – Eligibility of judicial officers to compete as against the post of District Judge by way of direct recruitment – Plea that practice as an advocate and service as a judicial officer for 10 years is to be treated at par as per explanation added to Arts. 124 & 217 – Held: In Rameshwar Dayal, this question has been considered and it was held that Art.233(2) could not be interpreted in view of the explanations added to Arts. 124 & 217.

Words & Phrases – "appointment", "advocates", "pleaders"
– Meaning of – Discussed – Constitution of India – Art.233.

• • •

CHAPTER LXII

INTERNET AND MOBILE ASSOCIATION OF INDIA Vs. RESERVE BANK OF INDIA, MARCH 04, 2020

Citations: (2020) 10 SCC 274

[R. F. NARIMAN, ANIRUDDHA BOSE AND V. RAMASUBRAMANIAN, JJ.]

Reserve Bank of India Act, 1934 – ss.17, 20-22, 26, 38, 45JA, 45L, 45U, 45W, 45Z-45ZO – Reserve Bank of India (RBI) issued a "Statement on Developmental and Regulatory Policies" dtd. 05.04.18 and circular dtd. 06.04.18 respectively, which directed the entities it regulated (i) not to deal with or provide services to any individual/business entities dealing with/ settling virtual currencies (VCs) and (ii) to exit the relationship, if they already have one, with such individuals/business entities – Challenged by petitioners (a specialized industry body representing interests of online & digital services industry; companies running online crypto assets exchange platforms; shareholders/founders thereof and individual crypto assets traders) inter alia on the ground that RBI has no power to prohibit the activity of trading in VCs through Virtual Currency Exchanges (VCEs) since they are not legal tender but tradable commodities/digital goods, not falling within the regulatory framework of 1934 Act or 1949 Act and that VCs do not even fall within the credit system of the country to enable RBI under the Preamble to 1934 Act giving it a mandate to operate the currency & credit system of the country to its advantage – Held: After 2016 Amendment Act, RBI is now vested with the obligation to operate the monetary policy framework in India – 1934 Act, 1949 Act and the 2007 Act cumulatively confer very wide powers upon RBI inter alia to operate the currency and credit system of the country to its advantage; regulate financial system of the country to its advantage; to issue directions to a payment system or a system participant which in RBI's opinion is engaging in any act that is likely to result in systemic risk being inadequately controlled or is likely to affect the payment system, monetary policy or the credit policy of the country and to issue directions to system providers or system participants or any other person generally, to regulate the payment systems or in the interest of management or operation of any of the payment systems or in public interest – Depending on the text of the statute involved in the case and the context, various courts in different jurisdictions have identified virtual currencies to belong to different categories ranging from property to commodity to non-traditional currency to payment instrument to money to funds – Petitioners' contention that VCs are just goods/commodities and can never be regarded as real money and that they are carrying on an activity over which RBI has no power statutorily, not accepted – Petitioners' contention that the impugned decision is ultra vires is rejected – Impugned Circular does not impose a prohibition on the use of/ trading in VCs, the prohibition is not per se against the trading in VCs – It is against banking companies, with respect to a class of transactions – Further, RBI cannot be held guilty of non-application of mind when the sequence of events from June 2013 up to 02-04- 2018 show that RBI was brooding over the issue for almost five years – Also, the contention that the impugned Circular is vitiated by malice in law and is a colorable exercise of power cannot be sustained – Impugned Circular cannot be assailed on the basis of M. S. Gill test either – It is no doubt true that RBI has very wide powers however, the availability of power is different from the manner and extent to which it can be exercised – RBI has not so far found, the activities of VCEs to have actually impacted adversely, the way the entities regulated by RBI function – When the consistent stand of RBI is that they have not banned VCs and when the Government of India is unable to take a call despite several committees coming up with several proposals including two draft bills, both of which advocated exactly opposite positions, it is not possible to hold that the impugned measure is proportionate –

Impugned Circular dtd. 06.04.18 is set aside on the ground of proportionality – Statement dtd. 05.04.18, though challenged, is not in the nature of a statutory direction and hence the question of setting aside the same does not arise – Finance Act, 2016 – Banking Regulation Act, 1949 – ss.5, 8, 21, 22, 27, 29A, 30(1B), 35AA, 35AB, 35A(1)(a), 36(1)(a), 36AA – Payment and Settlement Systems Act,

2007 – ss.2(1); 2(1)(g), (h), (i), (p) and ss.3, 4(1), 10(2), 11, 17, 18 – Administrative Law – Subordinate Legislation – Doctrine of Proportionality – Doctrine of Deference – Foreign Exchange Management Act, 1999 – ss.2(h), (i), (q) – Coinage Act, 2011 – Finance Act, 1994 – Finance Act, 2012 – Sales of Goods Act, 1930 – Central Foods and Services Tax Act, 2017 – s.2(75) – Constitution of India – Art.19(1)(g).

Reserve Bank of India Act, 1934 – Establishment of Reserve Bank of India – Object of – Discussed. Reserve Bank of India Act, 1934 – Preamble to; s.45L(1) – Held: Phrase "credit system of the country to its advantage", as found in paragraph 1 of the Preamble, is repeated in sub-sec. (1) of s.45L – Only difference between the two is that paragraph 1 of the Preamble speaks about the operation of the credit system, while s.45L (1) speaks about regulation of the credit system. Banking Regulation Act, 1949 – Power of Reserve Bank of India under – Discussed.

Reserve Bank of India Act, 1934 – s.3(1) – Held:

"management of the currency" appearing in s.3(1) need not necessarily be confined to the management of what is recognized in law to be currency but would also include what is capable of faking or playing the role of a currency. Payment and Settlement Systems Act, 2007 – Object of – Discussed.

Administrative Law – Colourable exercise of power & malice in law – Reserve Bank of India (RBI) issued circular directing the entities it regulated to not to deal with or provide services to any individual/business entities dealing with/settling virtual currencies (VCs) and to exit the relationship, if they have one, with such individuals/business entities – Petitioners contended that the invocation by RBI, of 'public interest' as a weapon, purportedly for the benefit of users, consumers or traders of virtual currencies is a colourable exercise of power – Held: Not tenable – Once it is conceded that RBI has powers to issue directions in public interest, it is impossible to exclude users, consumers or traders of virtual currencies from the coverage – To constitute colourable exercise of power, the act must have been done in bad faith and the power must have been exercised not with the object of protecting the regulated entities or the public in general, but with the object of hitting those who form the target – To constitute malice in law, the act must have been done wrongfully and willfully without reasonable or probable cause – Impugned Circular does not fall under the category of either of them. Administrative Law – Statutory Authority – Power of RBI and difference between another statutory creatures & RBI – Discussed.

Banking Regulation Act, 1949 – s.35A(1) – Reserve Bank of India (RBI) issued circular directing the entities it regulated to not to deal with or provide services to any individual/business entities dealing with/settling virtual currencies (VCs) and to exit the relationship, if they have one, with such individuals/business entities – Plea of the petitioners that expression 'public interest' appearing in s.35A(1)(a) cannot be given an expansive meaning – Held: Power u/s.35A to issue directions is to be exercised under four contingencies- (i) public interest (ii) interest of banking policy (iii interest of the depositors & (iv) interest of the banking company –

Expression "banking policy" is defined in s.5(ca) to mean any policy specified by RBI (i) in the interest of the banking system (ii) in the interest of monetary stability and (iii) sound economic growth – Public interest permeates all these three areas – This is why s.35A(1)(a) is invoked in the impugned Circular. Constitution of India – Art.19(1)(g) – Reserve Bank of India (RBI) issued circular directing the entities it regulated to not to deal with or provide services to any individual/business entities dealing with/settling virtual currencies (VCs) and to exit the relationship, if they have one, with such individuals/business entities – Plea of the petitioners (a specialized industry body representing interests of online & digital services industry; companies running online crypto assets exchange platforms; shareholders/founders thereof and crypto assets traders) that a total prohibition, especially through a subordinate legislation such as a directive from RBI, of an activity not declared by law to be unlawful, is violative of Art.19(1)(g – Held: Buying and selling of crypto currencies through VC Exchanges can be by way of hobby or as a trade/business – Persons who engage in buying and selling virtual currencies, just as a matter of hobby cannot pitch their claim on Art.19(1)(g), for what is covered herein are only profession, occupation, trade or business –Therefore hobbyists, who are one among the three categories of citizens (hobbyists, traders in VCs and VC Exchanges), straightaway go out of the challenge u/ Art.19(1)(g) – Second and third categories of citizens namely, those who have made the purchase and sale of VCs as their occupation or trade, and those who are running online platforms and VC exchanges can certainly pitch their claim on the basis of Art.19(1)(g).

Words & Phrases - "currency", "currency notes", "Indian currency" "money", "regulate" - Definition & Meaning of – Discussed.

• • •

CHAPTER LXIII

INDORE DEVELOPMENT AUTHORITY Vs. MANOHARLAL & ORS. ETC. MARCH 06, 2020

Citation: (2020) 8 SCC 129

[ARUN MISHRA, INDIRA BANERJEE, VINEET SARAN, M. R. SHAH AND S. RAVINDRA BHAT, JJ.]

Right to Fair Compensation and Transparency in Land Acquisition, Rehabilitation and Resettlement Act, 2013: Legislative history of the Act of 2013 – Purpose of its enactment – Salient features – Departure from old Land Acquisition Act in 2013 Act relating to Social Impact Assessment, Rehabilitation and Resettlement Scheme – Discussed.

Right to Fair Compensation and Transparency in Land Acquisition, Rehabilitation and Resettlement Act, 2013: s.24(2) –

Twin requirement for the lapse – Firstly, physical possession has not been taken and secondly compensation has not been paid – Whether the conditions are cumulative i.e. both are to be fulfilled for lapsing of acquisition proceedings or the conditions are in alternative ("either/or") – Held: s.24(2) of the Act of 2013 deals with a situation only where the award has been made five years or more before the commencement of the Act, but physical possession of the land has not been taken, nor compensation has been paid – As regards the collation of the words used in s.24(2), two negative conditions have been prescribed – General rule of statutory interpretation of positive and negative conditions are that positive conditions separated by 'or' are read in the alternative but negative conditions connected by 'or' are construed as cumulative and 'or' is read as 'nor' or 'and' i.e. the expression 'or' has to be read as conjunctive and conditions of both the clauses must be fulfilled – Thus, the word 'or' used in s.24(2) between possession and compensation has to be read as 'nor' or as 'and' – This would mean that the deemed lapse of land acquisition proceedings under s.24(2) takes place where due to inaction of authorities for five years or more prior to commencement of the Act of 2013, the possession of land has not been taken nor compensation has been paid – Thus, even if one condition is satisfied, there is no lapse – Interpretation of statutes.

Right to Fair Compensation and Transparency in Land Acquisition, Rehabilitation and Resettlement Act, 2013: s.24(2) –Interpreting "or" under s.24(2) of the Act of 2013 disjunctively –Effect of – Held: It would result in an anomalous situation, because, once compensation has been paid to the landowner, there is no provision for its refund – In case physical possession is with the landowner; and compensation has been paid, there is no provision in the Act for disgorging out the benefit of compensation – In the absence of any provision for refund in the Act of 2013, the State cannot recover compensation paid – The landowner would be unjustly enriched – This could never have been the legislative intent of enacting s.24(2) of the Act of 2013 – The principle of restitution, unless provided in the Act, cannot be resorted to by the authorities on their own – Absence of provision for refund in the Act of 2013 reinforces conclusion that the word "or" has to be read as conjunctively and has to be read as "and" – Doctrine of unjust enrichment and principle of restitution.

Right to Fair Compensation and Transparency in Land Acquisition, Rehabilitation and Resettlement Act, 2013: s.24(2) –

Purpose of – Held: To punish acquiring authority for its lethargy in not taking physical possession nor paying compensation after making award five years or more before commencement of Act of 2013 in pending proceedings providing they would lapse. Right to Fair Compensation and Transparency in Land Acquisition, Rehabilitation and Resettlement Act, 2013: s.24 – Vested right under – Held: s.24 of the Act of 2013 does not intend to take away vested rights – This is because there is no specific provision taking away or divesting title to the land, which had originally vested with the State, or divesting the title or interest of beneficiaries or third-party transferees of such land which they had lawfully acquired, through sales or transfers. Right to Fair Compensation and Transparency in Land s.24(2) – Whether proviso is part of s.24(2) or s.24(1)(b) – Held:

The proviso is part of the scheme of s.24(2) – The entire provision of s.24(2), including the proviso, operates when there is inaction for a period of five years or more, as contemplated therein.

Right to Fair Compensation and Transparency in Land Acquisition, Rehabilitation and Resettlement Act, 2013: s.24(2) –

Applicability to pending proceedings – Held: s.24(2) shall apply to the proceeding which is pending as on the date on which the Act of 2013, has been brought into force and it does not apply to the concluded proceedings – s.24(2) is not a tool to revive concluded proceedings and to question the validity of acquisition proceedings due to which possession were taken decades ago, or to question the manner of deposit of amount in the treasury – The Act of 2013 never intended revival of such claims – s.24(2) only contemplates lethargy/inaction of the authorities to act for five years or more.

Right to Fair Compensation and Transparency in Land Acquisition, Rehabilitation and Resettlement Act, 2013: s.24(2) – Whether gives rise to fresh cause of action – Held: s.24(2) of the Act of 2013 does not give rise to new cause of action to question the legality of concluded proceedings of land acquisition – s.24 does not revive stale and time-barred claims and does not reopen concluded proceedings nor allow landowners to question the legality of mode of taking possession to reopen proceedings or mode of deposit of compensation in the treasury instead of court to invalidate acquisition.

Right to Fair Compensation and Transparency in Land Acquisition, Rehabilitation and Resettlement Act, 2013: s.24(2) – Exclusion of period of interim order(s) – Held: Any court's interim order cannot be said to be inaction of the authorities or agencies; thus, time period is not to be included for counting the 5 years period as envisaged in s.24(2).

Right to Fair Compensation and Transparency in Land Acquisition, Rehabilitation and Resettlement Act, 2013: s.24(2) and its proviso – The expression 'paid' in the main part of s.24(2) does not include a deposit of compensation in court – The consequence of non-deposit is provided in proviso to s.24(2) in case it has not been deposited with respect to majority of land holdings then all beneficiaries (landowners) as on the date of notification for land acquisition under s.4 of the Act of 1894 shall be entitled to compensation in accordance with the provisions of the Act of 2013.

– In case the obligation under s.31 of the Act of 1894 has not been fulfilled, interest under s.34 of the said Act can be granted – Non deposit of compensation (in court) does not result in the lapse of land acquisition proceedings – In case of non- deposit with respect to the majority of holdings for five years or more, compensation under the Act of 2013 has to be paid to the "landowners" as on the date of notification for land acquisition under s.4 of the Act of 1894.

Right to Fair Compensation and Transparency in Land Acquisition, Rehabilitation and Resettlement Act, 2013: s.24(2) – When compensation, tendered, as provided in s.31(1) of the Act of 1894, but not paid/deposited in court – Whether acquisition lapse

– Held: In case a person has been tendered the compensation as provided under s.31(1) of the Act of 1894, it is not open to him to claim that acquisition has lapsed under s.24(2) due to non-payment or non-deposit of compensation in court – The obligation to pay is complete by tendering the amount under s.31(1) – Land owners who had refused to accept compensation or who sought reference

proceedings had lapsed under s.24(2) of the Act of 2013 – Land Acquisition Act, 1894 – s.31(1).

Land Acquisition: Mode of taking possession – When possession of large area of land is to be taken, then it is permissible to take possession by drawing Panchnama – Possession. comprises the right to possess and to exclude others, essential is animus possidendi – Possession depends upon the character of the thing which is possessed – If the land is not capable of any use, mere non-user of it does not lead to the inference that the owner is not in possession – The established principle is that the possession follows title – Possession comprises of the control over the property – The element of possession is the physical control or the power over the object and intention or will to exercise the power – Corpus and animus are both necessary and have to co-exist. Delay/laches: In matters of land acquisition, delay is fatal in questioning the land acquisition proceedings – In case possession has not been taken in accordance with law and vesting is not in accordance with s.16, proceedings before courts are to be initiated

within reasonable time, not after the lapse of several decades – Land Acquisition Act, 1894 – s.16. Interpretation of Statutes: Addition or substraction of word(s) in a statute – Power of Courts – Held: While interpreting the statutory provisions, addition or subtraction in the legislation is not permissible – It is not open to the court to either add or subtract a word – There cannot be any departure from the words of law, as observed in legal maxim "A Verbis Legis Non Est Recedendum" – Legal maxim.

Interpretation of Statutes: When two different expressions are used in the same provision of a statute, there is a presumption that they are not used in the same sense. Interpretation of statutes: Proviso to a provision – The function of the proviso is to explain or widen the scope – The proviso cannot travel beyond the provision to which it is attached.

Interpretation of Statutes: Colon (punctuation mark) –

Significance of its use – The use of the colon is to introduce a subclause that follows logically from the text before it – Right to Fair Compensation and Transparency in Land Acquisition, Rehabilitation and Resettlement Act, 2013 – s.24(2).

Judicial Notice: Judicial notice is taken of the fact that in no other Government security, rate of interest is higher on the amount being invested under ss.32 and 33 of the Act of 1894 – Higher rate of interest is available under s.34 to the advantage of landowners – Land Acquisition Act, 1894.

Repeal: Applicability of the General Clauses Act – Held: When repeal is followed by a fresh enactment on the same subject, the provisions of the General Clauses Act would undoubtedly require an examination of the language of the new enactment if it expresses an intent different from the earlier repealed Act – The enquiry would necessitate the examination if the old rights and liabilities are kept alive or whether the new Act manifests an intention to do away with or destroy them – If the new Act manifests different intentions, the application of the General Clauses Act will stand excluded – General Clauses Act.

Words and phrases: Word 'paid', tender', 'vesting' – Meaning of, discussed.

Words and phrases: Word 'paid' and 'deposited' – Distinction between – Dictionary meaning and meaning in the context of s.24(2) of Right to Fair Compensation and Transparency in Land Acquisition, Rehabilitation and Resettlement Act, 2013.

Words and phrases: Concept of vesting – Discussed.

• • •

CHAPTER LXIV

MADRAS BAR ASSOCIATION Vs. UNION OF INDIA & ANR. NOVEMBER 27, 2020

Citation: 2020(13) SCALE 443

[L. NAGESWARA RAO, HEMANT GUPTA AND S. RAVINDRA BHAT, JJ.]

Tribunal, Appellate Tribunal and other Authorities [Qualification, Experience and other conditions of service of Members] Rules, 2020 – National Tribunals Commission – Constitution of – Held: The Union of India directed to constitute a National Tribunals Commission which shall act as an independent body to supervise the appointments and functioning of Tribunals, as well as to conduct disciplinary proceedings against members of Tribunals and to take care of administrative and infrastructural needs of the Tribunals, in an appropriate manner – Till the National Tribunals Commission is constituted, a separate wing in the Ministry Finance, Government of India shall be established to cater to the requirements of the Tribunals.

Tribunal, Appellate Tribunal and other Authorities [Qualification, Experience and other conditions of service of Members] Rules, 2020 – Search-cum-Selection Committee – Composition of – Held: The Search-cum-Selection Committees should comprise of the following members: (i) The Chief Justice of India or his nominee—Chairperson (with a casting vote); (ii) The outgoing Chairman or Chairperson or President of the Tribunal in case of appointment of the Chairman or Chairperson or President of the Tribunal (or) the sitting Chairman or Chairperson or President of the Tribunal in case of appointment of other members of the Tribunal (or) a retired Judge of the Supreme Court of India or a retired Chief Justice of a High Court in case the Chairman or Chairperson or President of the Tribunal is not a Judicial member or if the Chairman or Chairperson or President of the Tribunal is seeking re-appointment—member; (iii) Secretary to the Ministry of Law and Justice, Government of India—member; (iv) Secretary to the Government of India from a department other than the parent or sponsoring department, nominated by the Cabinet Secretary–– member; (v) Secretary to the sponsoring or parent Ministry or Department—Member Secretary/

Convener (without a vote) – Till amendments are carried out, the 2020 Rules shall be read in the manner indicated – Further, r. 4(2) of the 2020 Rules shall be amended to provide that the Search-cum-Selection Committee shall recommend the name of one person for appointment to each post instead of a panel of two or three persons for appointment to each post.

Tribunal, Appellate Tribunal and other Authorities [Qualification, Experience and other conditions of service of Members] Rules, 2020 – rr.9(1) and 9(2) – Term of office of the Chairpersons, vice-chairpersons and the members of the Tribunal – Modification of the Rules, 2020 – Held: In view of the law laid down in the earlier judgments of the Supreme Court, the modification of the tenure is directed in rr. 9(1) and 9(2) of the 2020 Rules as five years in respect of Chairman or Chairperson, Vice Chairman or Vice-Chairperson and the members – The Government to amend r. 9 (1) of the 2020 Rules by making the term of Chairman, Chairperson or President as five years or till they attain 70 years, whichever is earlier and other members dealt with in r. 9(2) as five years or till they attain 67 years, whichever is earlier.

Tribunal, Appellate Tribunal and other Authorities [Qualification, Experience and other conditions of service of Members] Rules, 2020 – r. 15 – House Rent Allowance to the Chairperson and other members of the Tribunals – The lack of housing in Delhi has been one of the reasons for retired judges of the High Courts and the Supreme Court to not accept appointments

to Tribunals – Held: The Government of India directed to make serious efforts to provide suitable housing to the Chairperson and the members of the Tribunals and in case providing housing is not possible, to enhance the house rent allowance to Rs.1,25,000/- for members of Tribunals and Rs.1,50,000/- for the Chairman or Chairperson or President and Vice Chairman or Vice Chairperson or Vice President of Tribunals – In other words, an option should be given to the Chairperson and the members of the Tribunals to either apply for housing accommodation to be provided by the Government of India as per the existing rules or to accept the enhanced house rent allowance. Tribunal, Appellate Tribunal and other Authorities [Qualification, Experience and other conditions of service of Members] Rules, 2020 – Advocates as Judicial members – Held:

An Advocate of a High Court with experience of ten years is qualified for appointment as a Judge of the High Court as per Art. 217 (2) of the

Constitution of India – As the qualification for an advocate of a High Court for appointment as a Judge of a High Court is only 10 years, thus, the experience at the bar should be on the same lines for being considered for appointment as a judicial member of a Tribunal – However, it is left open to the Search-cum Selection Committee to take into account experience of the Advocates at the bar and the specialization of the Advocates in the relevant branch of law while considering them for appointment as judicial members.

Tribunal, Appellate Tribunal and other Authorities [Qualification, Experience and other conditions of service of Members] Rules, 2020 – Members of Indian Legal Service – Eligibility of – Held: The members of Indian Legal Service are entitled to be appointed only as technical members – The members of Indian Legal Service shall be entitled to be considered for appointment as a judicial member subject to their fulfilling the other criteria which advocates are subjected to – In addition, the nature of work done by the members of the Indian Legal Service and their specialization in the relevant branches of law shall be considered by the Search-cum-Selection Committee while evaluating their candidature.

Tribunal, Appellate Tribunal and other Authorities [Qualification, Experience and other conditions of service of Members] Rules, 2020 – Removal of members – r. 8 – Held: r. 8 of the Search-cum-Selection Committee in matters of disciplinary actions shall be final and the recommendations of the Search-cum Selection Committee shall be implemented by the Central Government. Tribunal, Appellate Tribunal and other Authorities [Qualification, Experience and other conditions of service of Members] Rules, 2020 – Time Limit for appointment – Held: The pendency of cases in the Tribunals is increasing mainly due to the lack of personnel in the Tribunals which is due to the delay in filling up the vacancies as and when they arise due to the retirement of the members – There is an imminent need for expediting the process of elections and appointments to ensure speedy justice – The Government of India directed to make the appointments to the Tribunals within three months after the Search-cum-Selection Committee completes the selection and makes its recommendations.

Tribunal, Appellate Tribunal and other Authorities [Qualification, Experience and other conditions of service of Members] Rules, 2020 – Retrospectivity of the 2020 Rules – The Government of India contended that the new Rules, 2020 have been framed in exercise of powers under the Finance Act, 2017, the 2020 Rules would be effective from 26.05.2017

– Held: The 2020 Rules which came into force from the date of their publication in the Official Gazette, i.e. 12.02.2020, cannot be given retrospective effect – The intention of Government of India to make the 2020 Rules prospective is very clear from the notification dated 12.02.2020 – In any event, subordinate legislation cannot be given retrospective effect unless the parent statute specifically provides for the same – It is clarified that all appointments made prior to the 2020 Rules which came into force on 12.02.2020 shall be governed by the parent Acts and Rules– Any appointment made after the 2020 Rules have come into force shall be in accordance with the 2020 Rules subject to the modifications directed in the preceding paragraphs of this judgment.

• • •

List Of Adv. Jayprakash Somani's Books

1. Supreme Court of India's Leading Case Laws on 'Insolvency & Bankruptcy Code 2016'
2. Bail Matters – Supreme Court's Latest Leading Case Laws
3. Arbitration Matters- Supreme Court's Latest Leading Case Laws
4. Property Matters - Supreme Court's Latest Leading Case Laws
5. Matrimonial Matters- Supreme Court's Latest Leading Case Laws
6. Election Matters- Supreme Court's Latest Leading Case Laws
7.SEBI Matters- Supreme Court's Latest Leading Case Laws
8. Banking Matters- Supreme Court's Latest Leading Case Laws
9. Service Matters- Supreme Court's Latest Leading Case Laws
10. Contempt of Court Matters- Supreme Court's Latest Leading Case Laws
11. Consumer Protection Matters- Supreme Court's Latest Leading Case Laws
12. Corporate Law- Supreme Court's Latest Leading Case Laws
13. Competition Act - Supreme Court's Latest Leading Case Laws
14. Armed Force Tribunal - Supreme Court's Latest Leading Case Laws
15. Acquittal From 376 - Supreme Court's Latest Leading Case Laws
16. Negotiable instrument – Supreme Court's Latest Leading Case Laws
17. Contract Act- Supreme Court's Latest Leading Case Laws
18. Supreme Court's AOR Exam- Leading Cases

• • •

These Books are available online at
Notion Press: https://notionpress.com/author/jayprakash_somani
Amazon: https://www.amazon.in/s?k=jayprakash+somani
Flipkart: https://www.flipkart.com/search?q=Jayprakash%20Somani

• • •

Videos & Tv Shows On Law & Exim

List of some important videos & TV shows on Law & EXIM by Adv. Jayprakash Somani on his YouTube Channel 'Jayprakash Somani EXIM & Legal'

Legal Videos: Hindi -English

1) SLP in Supreme Court / Special Leave Petitions in the Supreme Court of India

2) Transfer of Civil & Criminal Cases by the Supreme Court of India / Transfer of Matrimonial Cases

3) Appellate Jurisdiction of the Supreme Court of India

4) Jurisdictions of the Supreme Court of India

5) Public Interest Litigation in the Supreme Court of India / PIL in Supreme Court

6) Article 32 Writ Petitions in the Supreme Court of India

7) Bail Matters Top 10 Supreme Court Cases

8) FIR Quashing in High Court & Supreme Court

9) Bail & Anticipatory Bail Matters in Supreme Court

10) Insolvency & Bankruptcy Matters in the Supreme Court

11) Insolvency & Bankruptcy Code 2016 Part 1

12) Insolvency & Bankruptcy Code 2016 Part 2

13) Insolvency & Bankruptcy Code 2016 Part 3

14) Corporate Liquidation Process

15) Supreme Court Rules & Procedures Webinar of 2.5 hour on Zoom

16) RDDBFI Act, 1993 (Introduction)

17) The Indian Contact Act 1872

18) Negotiable Instruments Act (Introduction)

19) How to avoid matrimonial disputes& some more videos

20)SEBI Matters in the Supreme Court

21) Matrimonial Matters: Supreme Court's 20 Case Laws

22) Consumer Matters Supreme Court's 20 Case Laws

23) Service Matters Supreme Court's 20 Case Laws

24) How to Search Lawyer for Your Matter

25) Property Matters Supreme Court's 20 Case Laws

26) Bail Matters: Supreme Court's 20 Case Laws

27) Supreme Court / High Court Vacation Benches

28)69000 Teacher's Recruitment Matters of UP Government in the Supreme Court

29) Contempt of Court Matters in the Supreme Court

30) Advocate Act's Matters in the Supreme Court

31) Business Law Matters in the Supreme Court

32) Banking Matters in the Supreme Court

33) Labour Law Matters in the Supreme Court

34) Arbitration Matters in the Supreme Court

35) Careers in Law -Zoom Webinar by Adv. JayprakashSomani

36) Civil Matters in the Supreme Court

37) Consumer Protection Act | Consumer Matters in the Supreme Court

38) Corporate Matters in the Supreme Court

39) Criminal Matters in the Supreme Court

40) Role of Respondent in the Supreme Court of India

41) Motor Vehicle Accident Matters in Supreme Court with case laws

42) Article 131 Original Suits in Supreme Court

43)PIL in Supreme Court/ Public Interest Litigations in the Supreme Court of India'

44)CAB Citizenship Amendment Bill is not Unconstitutional

45) Supreme Court of India Cases & Process – Marathi

46) Legal Services Export / Export of Legal Services

47) Transfer of Matrimonial Cases by the Supreme Court of India

48) Public Interest Litigation PIL

49) The Specific Relief Act (Introduction)

50) Corporate Insolvency Resolution Process CIRP

51)ABMM's Career 5 - Careers in Law

52) Transfer of cases by Supreme Court

53) Writ Petitions in High Court & Supreme Court of India

54) Supreme Court Jurisdictions - Appeals, SLP, Writ Petitions, Transfer, Original, Review, Curative

55)LEGAL INDIA TV Show: Cases Handled in Supreme Court

56) Corporate Liquidation Process

57) Legal Services Export / Export of Legal Services

EXIM Videos: Hindi -English

1) Yes, I can do Import Export Business Easily! 36 points excellent video in Hindi

2) Yes, I can do Import Export Business Easily! 36 points excellent video in English

3) Import Export Business – Hindi video

4) Import Export Business - English video

5) Export Import Marathi TV Interview

6) Scope for Commerce Students in International Business- TV Show

7) Scope for Management Student in International Business- TV Show

8) Scope for Engineering Students in International Business – TV Show

9) Women in International Business- TV Show

10) How to do Import Export Business Successfully!'

11) Where one can get full information on Import Export Business?

12) What to do import & export?

13) Import Export Workshop/ Training/Course/ Diploma

14) How to Start Import Export Business & How to grow it. Live Webinar

15) Success Stories & Failure Stories in Import & Export Business

16) For MSME Scope in Export & Import...

17) Exports In Agri. & Food Products – English & some more videos

18) Exports to Dubai, Aabudhabii. e. UAE

19) Jewelry Exports from India

20) How to attend EXIM workshop to become excellent Exporter

21) Import Export Best Training Course – Online & Offline

22) Agri Product Export

23) Scope for Woman in International Business

24) Management Graduates Scope in International Business

25) Pharma Product's Export

26) Best Import Export Course | Practical Training | Aaronica Global Exim

27) Import Export Business for Commerce Graduates

28) How Do I Get Export Orders? Finding International Buyers

29) What Is APEDA In Import Export Business?

30) Which Is The Best Product To Export From India?

31)EXIM Remark by Manoj Kumar Faridabad

32)EXIM Remarks by Mahesh Telangana

33) What Licenses I Need To Start Import/ Export?

34) How Can I Increase My Import Export Business?

35) Which Is Best B2B Website For Import/Export Business?

36) Export Import Management with Global Marketing

37) How to Start Export Import Business | 51 Points Video

38) Scope for Commerce & Other Graduates in International Business

39)BE A SUCCESSFUL EXPORTER FOR OUR NATION - Marathi video

40) Export of Textile , Cotton, Agri., Food, & other products & services

41) Exports from MP, CG, MH, GJ & CA in Fresh Fruits & Vegetables

42) Exports in Agri. & Food Products- Hindi

43) Start your Online/E-Commerce Business

44) How to Start Export Import Business & Grow it

45) Exports in Textile & Other Products

46) Start and grow EXIM business - Live English Webinar

47)'Import Export Business!' Why, Who, What & How can one do it easily!!

48) Live: Export of Product & Services During & After Lock Down Period

49) Frauds in Import Export Business

50) Import Export for Business Man

51) Import & Export for Women

51) Import & Export for Graduate & Post - Graduate Students

52) Agriculture Exports from India

53) Digital Marketing Setup - Marathi

54)2nd Secret of Successful Businessman

55) Digital Marketing Set up

56) Legal Services Export / Export of Legal Services

57) Export & Import with UAE

58) Service Exports / Exports by Service Providers

59) Import Export Workshop/ Training/Course/ Diploma

60) Exports & Imports with USA

61) Selection on Product for Export

62) Top Products Exported from India

63) What to do import & export?

64)ABMM Career 2 - 'Careers in Business & Industries

65) How to do Import Export Business Successfully!'

66)5 Secrets of Successful Businessman

67) Export from MP, Chhattisgarh & Vidarbha Nagpur

68)EXIM Hindi - Textile & Apparel Export

69)EXIM Hindi - Export Import Practical Training In Delhi, Kolkata, Mumbai and Pune

70) Import Export Business

71) Import Export Business Hindi

72) Import Export Business English video

73) Import Export Business Marathi

74) Women in International Business by Exim Guru Adv. Jayprakash Somani

75) Opportunities in Foreign Trade- Adv. Jayprakash Somani's special interview

• • •

www.ingramcontent.com/pod-product-compliance
Ingram Content Group UK Ltd.
Pitfield, Milton Keynes, MK11 3LW, UK
UKHW021907190726
13853UKWH00002B/558

9 798885 214490